FORGIVENESS

AS THE WAY

...AND THE WAY
TO FORGIVENESS

ALBERTO ALMEIDA

FORGIVENESS
AS THE WAY ...AND THE WAY
WAY
TO FORGIVENESS

Jardim
das Oliveiras

ISBN 978-1-947179-54-7

Original title in Portuguese:
O Perdão como Caminho...e o Caminho do Perdão
(Brazil, 2012)

Authorized edition by Jardim das Oliveiras – Belem (PA) - Brazil

Published by Edicei of America
8425 Biscayne Boulevard Suite 104, Miami, FL 33138
Tel: (305) 758-7444 | fax: (305) 758-7449
E-mail: andreia.marshall@ediceiofamerica.com | Site: www.ediceiofamerica.com
Facebook: @EDICEIofAmerica | Twitter: @EdiceiofAmerica

For Jardim das Oliveiras
Passagem José de Alencar, Alameda Jardim Oliveira, 01. Castanheira. CEP 66645-030 – Belém/PA
Tel: +55 (91) 3119-2873 / 3245-1681
E-mail: jardim@jardimdasoliveiras.org | Site: www.jardimdasoliveiras.org
Facebook: @jardimdasoliveiras | Instagram: jardimoliveiras
Facebook: @albertoalmeidabelem | Instagram: alberto_almeida_belem

INTERNATIONAL DATA FOR CATALOGING IN PUBLICATION (ICP)

A447p   Almeida, Alberto

       Forgiveness as the way...And the way to forgiveness / Alberto Almeida. – 1. ed. – translated by Darrel Kimble – Miami (FL), USA : Edicei of America, 2018.

       148 p.; 21cm

       Original title: *O Perdão como Caminho...e o Caminho do Perdão*

       ISBN 978-1-947179-54-7

       1. Spiritism 2. Transpersonal Psychology 3. Forgiveness-Reflection. I. Title

                              CDD 133.9
                              CDU 173

CONTENTS

Introduction 7

CHAPTER 1
Concept: What Is Forgiveness?
And What Is It Not? 9

CHAPTER 2
Toxic Guilt and Rancor 15

CHAPTER 3
What Is behind (the Cause) of
Remorse and Rancor.................................... 23

CHAPTER 4
The Consequences of Not Forgiving............. 29
    4.1. Psycho-socio-emotional consequences ... 33
    4.2. Psycho-spiritual consequences 35
    4.3. Biological consequences....................... 36

CHAPTER 5
Love as the Foundation of Forgiveness 41

CHAPTER 6
Self-Forgiveness 49

CHAPTER 7
Forgiving Another Person 63

CHAPTER 8
Forgiving the Body and the
Body as Forgiveness 75

CHAPTER 9
Forgiveness of One's Parents.......................... 83

CHAPTER 10
Forgiveness of Children 93

CHAPTER 11
Forgiveness of a Spouse................................. 97

CHAPTER 12
Forgiveness of Enemies 105

CHAPTER 13
Forgiving and Forgetting............................ 109

CHAPTER 14
But What if I Just Cannot Forgive?............. 113

CHAPTER 15
...And the Way of Forgiveness.................... 121

INTRODUCTION

Love your enemies – Jesus.[1]

"FORGIVENESS AS THE WAY" is the title of a work that intends to offer forgiveness as a way of life, a means to existentially find our place in the world, since each and every day, life demands of us the art of loving just a little bit more in our quest to overcome our limitations as we progress toward our urgent self-enlightenment. It is obvious that continuously practicing love – the basis for the act of forgiving – is the great challenge set forth in this book.

With the subtitle "... and the way of forgiveness," the book aims to offer steps to achieve forgiveness promptly in light of each event that surfaces during our corporeal experience. In this regard, set phases are objectively outlined, didactically, to assist those who choose forgiveness when faced with a specific demand, such as forgiving a father, mother, child, spouse, enemy, etc.

It becomes clear that self-forgiveness* is the fundamental call for anyone who wants to forgive everything and everyone.

Self-forgiveness is an approach that includes a psychological/medical interface, and which is in line with the

---

[1] Matthew 5:44.

Spiritist vision – an approach derived from seminars held by the Spiritist Medical Association of Pará, and aimed at assisting individuals who are seeking to broaden their perspective regarding the transmutation*[2] of guilt and hurt into happy learning experiences, as well as preventing them from turning into remorse and rancor, and materializing in this lifetime or in others as physical infirmities, psychosocial/mental disorders, and spiritual disturbances, etc., requiring a major effort to solve problems that have become much more complex.

This is not a mystical or theological exegesis*, nor is it a strictly technical/academic study; it is an effort to share life contents that are just as important as *our daily bread.*[3]

The fundamental source for this simple offering may be found in the teachings of Jesus and Allan Kardec, together with professional experience in the areas of medicine and psychotherapy.

Because of the book's length, the publication of complementary material was postponed for later, by expanding and going into greater detail about Chapter 15 regarding the theory and practice of exercises capable of making "... the way of forgiveness" more feasible.

This work is merely the renewal of an invitation that has been repeated for two thousand years: ***Blessed are the merciful, for they will receive mercy.***[4]

ALBERTO RIBEIRO DE ALMEIDA
Belém, Brazil
February 10, 2012

---

[2] An asterisk indicates that the meaning of the word can be found in the Glossary at the end of the book.

[3] Matthew 6:11.

[4] Matthew 5:7.

CONCEPT: WHAT IS FORGIVENESS? AND WHAT IS IT NOT?

Father... forgive us our debts, as we forgive our debtors.[5]

When it comes to forgiveness, people usually do not grasp the real meaning of this virtue. They misrepresent its importance, either by giving it an overly transcendent, inaccessible character, or by trivializing it as something requiring very little effort, something very easy to do.

Everything depends on the way we look at forgiveness.

The viewpoint that sees forgiveness as something unattainable dehumanizes it, rendering it only an attribute of saints, thus distancing it from those who need it the most: evolving human beings. From this perspective, forgiveness cannot even be considered, since it is seemingly unobtainable.

---

[5] Matthew 6:12.

On the other hand, when forgiveness is trivialized, it is robbed of its virtue, or it becomes a mask*[6] that hides various weaknesses. In this case, forgiveness is just so many words spoken off-hand, superficially, where the heart does not take part.

But forgiveness is not anything like these two undesirable extremes. It is a virtue that requires continuous effort to implement, to make it capable of enabling human beings to go beyond themselves, such that it enlightens them for a revealing trans-humanization* about their nature as ever-ascending spiritual beings.

All this is so because forgiveness is a voyage rather than an arrival in port. It is also an act, but most of all, it is a life habit. It is a process, not just a circumstantial state of being.

Its very etymology[7] translates its meaning. It comes from the Latin *perdonare; per-*, "total, complete," and *donare*, "to give, hand over, donate."

Much like the [Portuguese] words *pernoitar* (to stay all night) and *percurso* (to travel the path all the way), forgiveness suggests an all-giving, a complete pathway entailing a handing over.

To forgive, therefore, means to take a pathway of love for as long as needed to resolve an instance of rancor and/or remorse. Love is the substrate, the raw material of forgiveness.

---

[6] An asterisk indicates that the meaning of the word can be found in the Glossary at the end of the book.

[7] The English word *forgive* is from the Old English *forgiefnes, forgifennys*, which means *pardon*. The word in the original Portuguese text is *perdão* (which in most instances, we have translated into the more common English word *forgiveness*), the cognate of the English word *pardon*, both coming from the Latin *perdonare,* as the paragraph explains. In the original Portuguese, this paragraph, of course, refers to the etymology of the Portuguese term *perdão*. – Tr.

Fundamentally, to forgive means to be challenged to show love-compassion in the act of giving. In order to be eliminated, rancor and/or toxic guilt requires a quota (dose) of love that overcomes the amount of suffering.

On a scale of zero to 10, metaphorically speaking, if you show love on a level of 05, you will not become resentful or blame yourself when these two emotions are below that level, for example, 03 or 04. However, if the need requires a level of 06, then you will not be able to forgive; you will need time to improve your score, your amount of love, to reach at least 06. And to get there, you will need to put time and effort into practicing love to overcome the presented requirement.

That is why Jesus stated: **"And whoever compels you to go one mile, go with him two"**[8]; **"And if someone takes your cloak, do not refuse him your tunic."**[9] To forgive means to love beyond what is necessary; it means to cover the demand, to give more love than requested.

For this path to be completed and forgiveness be put into effect, it might take, for example, one minute, one day, one week, one month, a year, a decade, a whole lifetime... or many lifetimes, depending on three variables: the severity of the offense, the willingness to forgive, and the ability to love.

a) The severity of the offense

In the material, literal sense, there are different degrees of severity when it comes to wrongs: the destruction of a glass, a TV, a car, a house. The same applies at the existential level...

However, the offense is always relative to the meaning we attach to the pain it causes because the same

---

[8] Matthew 5:41.

[9] Luke 6:29.

harmful event may be factored differently, depending on the assessment of the one who experiences the suffering. What might be only slight harm for one person may be regarded as cruelty by another.

b) The ability to love

The current ability to love and the willingness to expand this sentiment make forgiveness possible, thus shortening the time of conflict.

c) The willingness to forgive

The desire and the will to mobilize a greater amount of love to face the limitation imposed by the hurt and/or guilt help determine how long it will take us to overcome our own limitations and continue following the path of forgiveness.

Thus, according to these three factors – size of the offense, level of accumulated love, and willingness to forgive – we either stagnate on the road of life and remain fixed in pain, or we advance, transmuting our suffering into a learning experience and taking a loving pathway until we arrive at the door of our own liberation.

* * *

To sum up: Forgiveness is not for the archangels. They have already enlightened themselves through love. Forgiveness is a path of growth for those who need to learn to love a little more.

Forgiveness is not an attitude of appearances, stamped with pretty words meant to gain social praise. Forgiveness is a commitment to our own conscience in order to achieve inner peace.

Forgiveness is not connivance* with our own wrong (or someone else's). Rather, it means taking responsibility for the wrong and righting it.

Forgiveness is not an outward manifestation lacking learning, sought magically. Forgiveness is a journey inward, toward the heart itself, in order to accomplish it at the expense of continuous effort.

Forgiveness is also an arrival station; but above all, it is the means to reach the terminal. Therefore, it is a pathway along which we advance every day, to one day arrive at... the door of our own illumination.

CHAPTER 2

TOXIC GUILT AND RANCOR

*Hypocrite! First remove the beam from your own
eye, and then you can see (in depth) to remove the
speck from your brother's eye.*[10]

Guilt and hurt are the two sides opposed to forgiveness.

Basically, remorse is aggressiveness directed at oneself;
rancor, toward someone else.

Remorse speaks of a transgression against divine law
when we act to the detriment of someone or of something,
causing suffering or disharmony outside of ourselves, but with
like reflection for our own conscience.

In identical circumstances, on the other hand, it also
happens when someone acts to harm us, causing us suffering
or harm. That is when rancor may take root against someone
who has also violated the law of love.

The remedy is self-forgiveness and hetero-forgiveness*,
respectively, for guiltiness and resentment.

---

[10] Matthew 7:5.

When the spirit dwells on guilt, the result is undesirable, harmful remorse for the one who harbors it, for it comprises toxic guilt.

Guilt is only desirable when it is expressed as repentance, that is, "coming to one's senses," "taking responsibility for," thus making room for a new movement of the soul toward reparative action.

However, at the opposite end to the toxic cultivation of guilt are persons who fail to get in touch with it, even seriously deceiving themselves. They are not bothered at all by their wrongs, and this can reveal the presence of a sociopathy characterized by a highly complex mental disorder.

* * *

Reconcile yourself[11]... *with your adversary quickly, while you are on the road with him, so that he will not hand you over to the judge, and the judge hand you over to the officer, who will throw you into prison. Verily I say to you that you will not be released until you have paid the last cent*[12] is Jesus' warning to those who wish to live in harmony, free of the bitter burden of guilt and/or hurt.

The sentence is crystal clear. It is divided into two very distinct movements.

---

[11] The word in the original Greek is transliterated as *diallogethi*, which is the middle voice of the verb *diallassomai*. The middle voice in Greek is the same as the reflexive in Portuguese, which the Portuguese version of the Bible, used by the author, translates as "Reconcilia-te," literally "Reconcile yourself," but which is translated in English versions, such as the New American Standard Version, as "Be reconciled to." However, in order to get the author's argument across, we have retained the form of the Portuguese verb. – Tr.

[12] Matthew 5:24-26.

* * *

The first movement: *Reconcile YOURSELF...* is the part that falls to us to the degree that we want to pursue the path of forgiveness. It is a call for us to do our part, the part that concerns only ourselves, independently of the person with whom we are in conflict.

This step speaks of our relationship with ourselves, of our inner work apart from the other person, who is merely a mirror in which we see ourselves. It points to the fact that it is up to us what only we ourselves can achieve: self-forgiveness.

This path is individual, non-transferable, inalienable. It is traveled whether our adversary is aware of it or not, agrees to it or not, is near or far away. It all depends solely on us. It is the work of self-reconciliation, of self-love, and it sometimes takes a long time to build self-forgiveness, the generator of inner peace.

Thus, it means treating the remorse and/or rancor that weighs so heavily on us.

* * *

Still within the first movement, going deeper and aiming at a didactic analysis, let us focus exclusively on guilt.

The gospel quote – *Reconcile YOURSELF* – reveals that we habitually commit wrongs (attempts at learning), since the call is not restricted to conciliation only, but entails re-conciliation, implying that our offenses recur.

It is important to know if there are limits to our repeating errors that end up imputing remorse.

The answer lies in the question Peter asked of Christ:

"How many times shall my brother sin against me and I forgive him? Up to seven times?"[13]

That was as far as he could go in forgiving someone: seven times. But since the truth is a two-way street, that was also the number of times Peter would need the forgiveness of others.

Taking himself as a reference, Peter meant that he would be able to forgive as many as seven times, as if to suggest unconsciously that he would err seven times at most, thus requiring an equal number of pardons by others and, by extension, self-pardons, to actualize the *reconcile YOURSELF*.

The Master, however, demonstrated how much Peter did not know about himself, because he thought he was setting a very bold limit for himself. The Master makes a new proposal for Peter's arithmetic of forgiveness:

"Jesus said to him: Not seven times, but seventy times seven."[14]

And Jesus was right, for at the house of the high priest, Peter would deny his Master three times, not to mention the times leading up to the arrest, because he went to sleep more than once on the Mount of Olives, and, when he woke up, he wounded the ear of the high priest's slave who was with the group arresting Christ, in direct contradiction to the teachings of meekness and mildness he had received from Him.

Knowing that human beings are weak, Jesus takes advantage of the incident to propose *seventy times seven*, indicating the recurrent nature of fallibility that characterizes humanity still at a level of precarious evolution.

Moreover, He makes it implicit that we, Peter-humans, would not only need to forgive *seventy times seven*, but that,

---

[13]   Matthew 18:21.
[14]   Matthew 18:22.

above all, we are capable of committing just as many offenses,[15] needing the ongoing forgiveness of others.

This implies that we can deduce another teaching from Jesus, requiring a closer examination of everyday life:

– How many times, for the same reason, have we exploded in anger at a loved one, thus being in need of repeated forgiveness?

– How many sickly instances of jealousy, hurting a loved one, have made us beg for countless pardons?

– How many repeated episodes of abusing our body, by ingesting reportedly harmful substances, have made us ask our brain for successive pardons?

– How many vices, affecting our health by damaging our biological balance, have made us reiterate pleas for mercy from our body?

– How many troubles because of a lack of camaraderie with co-workers have required renewed apologies from us?

In the end it seems we need *seventy times seven pardons* for EACH WEAK AREA in our lives. Since we repeat THE SAME OFFENSES, we face the same tests over and over... until the lesson finally takes hold.

Therefore, whether it be guilt or hurt, *reconcile YOURSELF* means that we need to do our part in a conflict and take responsibility for our share, without transferring it to or passing it off on someone else, since we usually project* our problems onto other people (adversary, father, mother, son, friend, etc.), or onto the stars, spirits, bad luck, our profession, our city, God...

* * *

---

[15] *O Consolador*, response no. 338 (Dictated by the Spirit Emmanuel, through the medium Francisco Candido Xavier, Brazilian Spiritist Federation, 1940).

The second movement: *reconcile yourself...* WITH YOUR ADVERSARY.

This is when another person whom we feel has offended us (rancor), or whom we have offended (remorse), enters on the scene.

The *adversary* may be a person (spouse, father, mother, son, other family member, business partner, neighbor, etc.), but can also be a thing (our body, a country, a profession, a doctrine, etc.).

This is the moment when our relationship with our *adversary* comes into play; that is, a moment of contact with him or her. Thus, it requires us to actually seek out the other person in order to establish the second stage of the reconciliation.

This is how to handle the hurt found in relationships as an aggressive-destructive energy, entailing names and varying shades: anger, resentment, hatred, rage, etc.; or else it addresses the guiltiness that appears with tonalities known by the names of remorse, regret, compunction*, contrition, etc.

At this point we need to interact with the one who occupies the position of *adversary*. It is the act of going to meet the other person and it requires his or her participation and complicity to effect complete forgiveness.

Of course success at this step also depends on the other because he or she is called to actively participate in the construction of forgiveness by "offering his or her hand." It is the bringing of two into solidarity, partnership.

If both parties are amenable to an alliance, an accord, then a journey of forgiveness (*"while you are on the road with him"*) will take place until the ties of suffering are undone, with the dissolution of hurt/guilt and the (re)establishment of the bonds of harmony and peace.

If the other protagonist rejects the meeting, however, and avoids contact because he or she is not yet receptive to a reconciliation, then let us be the one whose conscience is at peace since, after being reconciled with our own self, we dared to go to meet our brother or sister to effect forgiveness by seeking the fair solution to the offense.

Therefore, let us respect the other person's will* if he or she decides to avoid the reunion for whatever reason... Since it is not our place to violate anyone's will, we must remain silent, for we have done our part, and can be at peace.

In doing the second movement, we thus free ourselves from the rancor and/or remorse, and we find forgiveness internally, with or without the other person's participation.

In doing so, the presence of the *judge* (our conscience) or the *officer* (good spirits) will not be needed in the future, nor will *prison* (a new body, a new incarnation) for the settlement of disputes that had fallen by the wayside.

CHAPTER 3

WHAT IS BEHIND (THE CAUSE) OF REMORSE AND RANCOR

Woe to you, scribes and Pharisees, hypocrites. You are like whitewashed sepulchers: showy on the outside, but full of dead bones and filthy on the inside.[16]

What is the greatest obstacle to progress? Answer: pride and selfishness.[17]

Pride and selfishness are the two giants that structure the matrices from which remorse and rancor arise, keeping us from moving forward.

Pride egoically* reflects the insecurity, low self-esteem*, unworthiness, the weakness that persons feel they possess.

Selfishness* manifests a lack, for which the soul seeks compensation* from the outside in, by resorting to things

---

[16] Matthew 23:27.

[17] *The Spirits' Book,* question 785. (Kardec, Allan. *The Spirits' Book,* International Spiritist Council, fourth edition, 2010)

and people that the soul feels should revolve around its ego*, which is poor, empty, hungry.

Consequently, the spirits are categorical, stating:

Let all of you, therefore, make every effort to fight selfishness within you, for that monster that devours all minds, that child of pride, is the source of all the miseries of this world.[18]

These are the solutions to related problems, clearly spelled out: *Charity and humility: that is the sole path to salvation; selfishness and pride: that is the sole path to perdition. This principle is formulated in precise terms in these words: "You shall love God with all your soul and your neighbor as yourself."*[19]

* * *

Sin is well-conceived in ancient Greek as "hamartia" which, translated, means "to err," "to miss the mark." Sinning is an error of orientation; it means to make an attempt, a try, and miss. Therefore, it may be a form of learning by means of what not to do, thus accumulating more experience.

From the Spiritist perspective, the spirit makes its evolutionary periplus*, by the continuous expansion of its divine potential, mediated through reincarnations. During each incarnation, the spirit makes use of an ego that structures a personality by which it will live in contact with the physical world, society, and people individually, experiencing and expanding its spiritual heritage in the eternal becoming.

---

[18] *The Gospel according to Spiritism,* chap; XI, no. 11 (Kardec, Allan. *The Gospel according to Spiritism,* International Spiritist Council, 2008).

[19] Ibid. chap. XV, no. 5.

It is through these relationships that the spirit's inner light, derived from the Creator Himself, will bloom, thus following its evolutionary trajectory from *the primitive atom to the archangel, who also began as only an atom.*[20]

In this ongoing coming to transcend, impasses arise between the ego, representing the human personality during each incarnation, and its spiritual essence, manifested as a *flame, a glow, or an ethereal spark...*"[21] The struggle between the human and the spiritual, the ego and the ethereal spark, the personality and the transcendent dimension, the transitory and the eternal light, is normal.

Therein lies the foundation of our greatest existential conflicts throughout our reincarnations.

If the ego closes itself off from the inner Christ, the being becomes fragmented and an evolutionary mismatch arises, since the person is weakened and starts sinning, that is, missing the mark.

When the human self (ego) dominates the scene on the stage of life by controlling the existential script, "egocentrism" is the result instead of "Christocentrism." In this situation, by-products of the ego manifest: egomania*, egotism*, selfishness, pride, etc.

If the ego yields to the higher SELF (ethereal spark),[22] life flows and the individual evolves without suffering. Here, the god within guides the ego which submits to it, enabling the following by-products to unfold: self-love, love for others, love for the earth; charity, altruism, etc.

---

[20] *The Spirits' Book,* response to question 540.

[21] Ibid. Question 88.

[22] *Momentos de Meditação,* chap. 4, by the Spirit Joanna de Ângelis, through the medium Divaldo Pereira Franco, Leal Publisher, 2014).

Almost all human suffering stems from the personality prevailing over the SELF (the spark) within.

When the interests of the hyperinflated ego are thwarted, hurt can result; and even when such interests are met, since they do not confer plenitude on their possessor, they generate discomfort and pain instead.

Thus, in daily life, we can witness persons with wounded egoic susceptibility when someone: says no to their whim; does not invite them to an important event; does not return their affection; betrays their trust; steals something from them; disappoints their friendship; proves ungrateful; excludes them from a group; does not pay them a favor; does not repay some money, etc.

In view of these attitudes, which may entail either involuntary/unconscious or deliberately conscious actions, such individuals may feel hurt if they choose to react egoically, instead of acting from the inner Christ that speaks of our divine nature.

The same process occurs with the appearance of toxic guilt, since it is the ego – the generator and maintainer of selfishness and pride, proving itself unable to accept and embrace its own offense, its defeat, its disappointment with itself – which reacts with devastating remorse.

Hence, in everyday life we can witness individuals with a fragile egoic manifestation being deeply affected by having to face the negative results of their own actions, their abusive and violent behaviors, their betrayals and lies, their extortions and manipulations, their envy and jealousy, their hatred and revenge, etc.

Consequently, it is appropriate to quote Fenelon:

Selfishness is founded on the importance of the personality. When well understood, I repeat, Spiritism enables you to see things from such an evolved point of view that the sentiment of the personality somehow disappears, so to speak, before the immensity of it all. Upon destroying this self-importance, or, at least, showing it for what it is worth, Spiritism necessarily combats selfishness.[23]

When they rightly understand that selfishness is one of those causes; that it engenders the pride, ambition, cupidity*, envy, hatred and jealousy of which they are at every moment the victim; that it brings trouble into all social relations, provokes dissension and destroys trust, obligating them to constantly maintain a defensive attitude toward their neighbor; that it engenders a sentiment that converts friend into foe, then they will also understand that this vice is incompatible with their own happiness… Thus, the more they suffer as a result of it, the more they will feel the need to fight it as they would a plague, harmful animals and all other scourges. They will be compelled to do so out of their own self-interest. [24]

When people live from the inner Christ guiding the ego, there is no room for guilt or resentment, because it monitors their moral conduct regarding selfishness and pride, those foundations of invasive hurt and guilt.

Rancor and remorse only arise when people act from an ego disconnected from the inner Christ. And only when they reconnect with God within, can they forgive themselves and others.

---

[23] *The Spirits' Book,* response to question 917.

[24] *The Spirits' Book,* comment on response to question 917.

CHAPTER 4

THE CONSEQUENCES OF NOT FORGIVING

And not one of them (sparrows) will fall to the ground without your Father's [consent]. All the hairs on your head are numbered. So, fear not. You are worth more than many sparrows.[25]

When modern physics presents its studies on the nature of matter and the field concept, it comes close to what Spiritism teaches through its studies of the spirit and the fluids.

Matter is a manifestation of condensed energy, according to high-energy physics.

The Spirits very appropriately informed Allan Kardec: **...matter also exists in states that are unfamiliar[26] ...what you term a molecule is still very far from being the elementary molecule[27] ...What appears to you to be a void is actually**

---

[25] Matthew 10: 29 – 31.

[26] *The Spirits' Book,* response no. 22.

[27] Ibid. response no. 34.

occupied by matter that cannot be detected by your senses or instruments.[28]

In addition to the field concept theorized by modern physics, Spiritism reveals the fluidic atmosphere formed from the fluids emitted by the spirit through its spirit body – the perispirit* – affecting the material, physical body and its existential environment.

These fluids faithfully express what we are inwardly in the cultivation of our thoughts and sentiments, thus depicting our secret, innermost reality.

Allan Kardec writes: **Since these fluids are the vehicle for thought, which can modify their properties, it is obvious that they must be impregnated with the good or bad qualities of the thoughts that set them in motion, and they change according to the purity or impurity of sentiments.**

(...) From a moral point of view, they bear the mark of the sentiments of hate, envy, jealousy, pride, selfishness, violence, hypocrisy, goodness, benevolence, love, charity, tenderness, etc. (...) A table of the fluids would thus contain all the passions, virtues and vices of humankind, and all the properties of matter corresponding to the effects they produce.

...it (the perispirit) in turn, reacts upon the physical organism, with which it is in molecular contact. If its emanations are good in nature, the body gets a healthy feeling from them; if they are [bad], the feeling is painful. If the [bad] emanations are continuous and fierce, they can cause physical disorders; certain diseases have no other cause.[29]

---

[28] Ibid. response no. 36.

[29] *Genesis*, chap. XIV, nos. 16, 17 and 18 (Kardec, Allan, *Genesis*. International Spiritist Council, 2009).

Forgiveness at this level of expression tells of the inner dynamics of our being, affecting, especially through the perispiritual property of emission-absorption, those with whom we become entangled in the web of remorse and/or rancor, in such a way that, due to the law of attunement, we can be perceived by other persons.

Thus we can see that we are immersed in a web of energy, and that a tree cannot be burned without affecting the whole forest, nor can a rose garden be destroyed without affecting a constellation of stars; that there is a close connection between the brain and the heart, as well as between thought and molecule, feeling and cell, forgiveness and health. (See the end of the chapter "The Dynamics of Guilt – Hurt Dealt with by the Ego").

* * *

During a psychotherapeutic session, Maria was dealing with a love relationship that had ended more than two years ago, but due to the hard feelings resulting from the experience, emotionally it had not yet ended for her.

The session was activating too many painful memories evoked with tears of resentment for all that she had suffered at the hands of her former partner, despite the fact that she was now married to another man and had not been in contact with her ex since he had left town two years ago.

When the session ended, she was greatly surprised when she checked her cell phone: in her voice-mail there was a message with a call she had received from her ex at the exact moment that she was undergoing her emotional catharsis*.

She was startled and wondered if her thoughts and feelings could have affected him more than two thousand miles away because she had not communicated with him since he had moved away.

Fifteen days later, in similar circumstances during another therapy session, the subject was treated with the same emotional intensity, bringing still-present hard feelings to light.

And what seemed to have been a coincidence happened again: her ex called again during the session and left a message on her voice-mail, even though he had not received a response to his previous call since Maria had chosen to ignore it.

Such events are repeated every day either overtly or subtly, revealing that energetic – fluidic – world in which we are immersed and systemically connected, regardless of physical distance and time, whether in the body or out of it.

When we hate, we affect other persons, who will feel resentful if they are on the same vibrational wavelength because our "call" reverberates when there is attunement.

However, if our harmful energy – from resentment and/or guilt – can reach and infect individuals who are physically far away but in tune with our maleficence, then what about the harmful effects on our own body, which is closer to us than our closest neighbor?

What happens to those who pour acid into their own hands to fling it on someone else, hoping to get revenge?

Following the same principle, when we forgive, we do not just reach those who let themselves be touched by our love when they consent to it, such that a symphony of the good resounds in their soul, but also, and above all, our own biological instrument is reached with the loving energy that we put into the act of forgiving.

Forgiveness is an energetic act.

Similar to the light that shines in the nighttime darkness, which, besides brightly illuminating its place of origin, also reaches someone who sees it through the window of an airplane more than 36,000 feet up, forgiveness triggers vibrant fluids that can create a vibratory field that rebounds from its originator to people and areas far, far away.

Forgiveness beneficially impacts mainly the epicenter* where it originates; however, it is not limited to the person who generates it, but radiates outward as an offering to everyone around who choose to enjoy it, like a flower bud, which, upon opening, perfumes itself and then spreads its fragrance unconditionally not only to the hummingbird flitting in the sky, but to the swamp tied to the land. (See the end of the chapter "The Dynamics of Guilt – Hurt Dealt with by the SELF")

4.1. PSYCHO-SOCIO-EMOTIONAL CONSEQUENCES

If your brother sins against you, discuss the matter with him in private.[30]

The repercussions of rancor and/or guilt that poison a person at the psychological level may be confined to the emotions, or they may reach the most refined level of the mental field, throwing the psychic structure into disarray.

Regarding the emotions, rancor and/or guilt manifests through egoic difficulty as it affects interpersonal relationships due to the accumulation of emotional garbage it brings to social interactions.

Any suppressed resentment and/or remorse affects communication in that, as a means of transferring their inner disarray, such individuals have difficulty in interacting not only with persons with whom they are having problems, but also with social relations in general.

---

[30] Matthew 18:15.

Thus there are noisy silences, excessive aggression, superiority complexes, baseless sadness, exaggerated fear, perfectionism, self-pity, inferiority complexes, pettiness, scolding, harmful distancing or invasive approaches, etc. All these reveal content that has not been sorted out properly because it was "swept under the rug" and, as such, it shows up in one's daily life, or it erupts abruptly and causes great damage.

The untreated problem (rancor/guilt) acts consciously and unconsciously in a negative way in one's life, generating various conflicts.

So many individuals display true psychological profiles due to retained guilt and/or accumulated hurt, including:

– Men who are violent because they piled up hard feelings in childhood;

– Women who are depressed for not having gotten over post-abortion guilt;

– Teenagers who are rebellious because of untold resentment for being put down by their parents;

– Elderly persons who are bitter since they have not been able to release from their heart the guilt stored up over a lifetime;

– People bearing much hurt accumulated day by day;

– Spouses with pathological jealousy after unforgiven betrayal;

– Parents who are overly anxious because they regret not having been successful at rearing their children;

– Children who are sad for not coming to grips with their pain/resentment from having been neglected by lax parents.

And lastly, people of all ages and social classes, educated and uneducated, religious or not, who bear the heavy burden of bitterness, depression, fear, intolerance, hatred, inflexibility, etc., for carrying guilt and/or hard feelings as generators and nourishers of such behaviors.

However, guilt, like resentment, can become so serious that it can affect one's mental dynamics and compromise their functionality, from simple manifestations to psychiatric disorders.

Therefore, not being able to forgive can affect, albeit in a simple form, one or more of the mental functions: thinking, memory, concentration, attention, affection, good judgment, intelligence, etc.

In terms of greater complexity, intense remorse and/or rancor can structure various pathologies in the vast chapter of psychiatry in this lifetime or a future one; for example, personality and behavior disorders, anxiety and mood disorders, or even the most serious disruptions, such as schizophrenia and autism.

4.2: PSYCHO-SPIRITUAL CONSEQUENCES

Jesus said to them (the disciples): this kind (of spirit) will only come out by prayer...[31]

Plutonium*, cesium* and uranium* are feared for their levels of radioactivity, which can mortally harm anyone who handles or gets near them. But we are far from measuring the deadly power of remorse and hurt for those who retain them in their soul, spreading harmful effects to all who tune in to their destructive frequencies.

Everything is attunement in the universe.

Holding on to harmful residues such as resentment and guilt is the same as fermenting toxic waste and exhaling miasmas*, attracting equal affinities to establish symbioses* similar to those between putrid debris and gadflies, landfills and vultures.

We need only evaluate what we cultivate concerning *hard feelings* and we will be able to tell what types of spirits we

---

[31] Mark 9:29.

attract as potential obsessors: animosity attunes us with hostile entities; anger connects us with violent spirits; hatred beacons to ruthless sicarios*; revenge incites murderous spirits...

Under like circumstances, cultivating *remorse* can entail a connection with unhappy spirits, leading to obsessions that reinforce guilt or induce other pitiable states such as self-loathing, self-condemnation, self-punishment, depression ... thoughts of suicide.

It is not enough just to hold obsessors at bay by trying to blame them as the cause behind our psycho-spiritual disasters: *it does no good to swat at the flies; it is necessary to heal the wound.*

Therefore, the task is one of self-evangelization to heal the wounds of our mental house through forgiveness, thus filling our soul with love, since, as Jesus stated, **"Now when an unclean spirit leaves a man, it goes through arid places, seeking rest but not finding it. Then it says, 'I will return to the house from which I came'. When it arrives, it finds the place empty, swept and well-furnished. So it leaves and brings back seven other spirits more wicked than itself, and they enter and dwell there. And the last (state) of that man becomes worse than the first."**[32]

4.3. BIOLOGICAL CONSEQUENCES

See, you have become sane. Sin no longer or something worse might happen to you.[33]

We are still far from assessing the full extent of the consequences of not forgiving.

---

[32] Matthew 12:43-45.

[33] John 5:14

Every psychological attitude of lengthy fixation in the cultivation of guilt or hurt leads not only to the above-mentioned psycho-affective changes, but also to energy dystonias* that inevitably affect the body in this or other incarnations. (See the table at the end of chapter 8 "Morbid Predisposition and Microbial Invasion").

The psycho-emotional disorders of the spirit act on the perispirit, which suffers because of the poor quality of the thoughts and of the emotions filled with remorse and/or rancor.

The perispirit, affected in areas where the mind is unbalanced, affects the vital fluid (the etheric double) and, consequently, the harmony of the body, at first as a mere subjective feeling of discomfort, then as bodily dysfunction, and ultimately as a full-blown harmful alteration.

Illnesses appear with infectious features (viruses, bacteria, fungi, etc.) as degenerative processes, congenital* manifestations, autoimmune disorders and other pathological forms, like a sewer that drains from the subtle field (spiritual body) to the biological body (physical body), toward the health of the soul (search for forgiveness). Thus starting or ending a long journey of forgiveness – depending on whether the issue involves, respectively, a rebellious and recalcitrant spirit, or someone who, even though having made a reasonable journey toward forgiveness, failed to prevent the materialization of residual guilt/resentment (infirmity) due to not having achieved, in a timely manner, the total transmutation of suffering into a learning experience through love-mercy.

The former (rebellious and stubborn) are just beginning their journey toward forgiveness; hence the infirmity represents bitter, expiatory suffering, which will be followed by other equally challenging phases.

The latter (less resistant, more amenable) use the infirmity to finalize the liberating process, earning the right to be free again and to progress less hindered toward the Creator.

Therefore, only those who practice love can avoid these organic effects (infirmities) because they have eliminated hostility and hatred of others, as well as their own shortcomings and guilt by way of love-forgiveness, transforming their troubles into learning experiences long before their consequences affect their organic garb. They can avoid the pedagogical infirmity because they availed themselves of the **love that covers a multitude of sins.**[34]

---

[34] 1 Peter 4:8.

The Dynamics of Guilt – Hurt Dealt with by the EGO

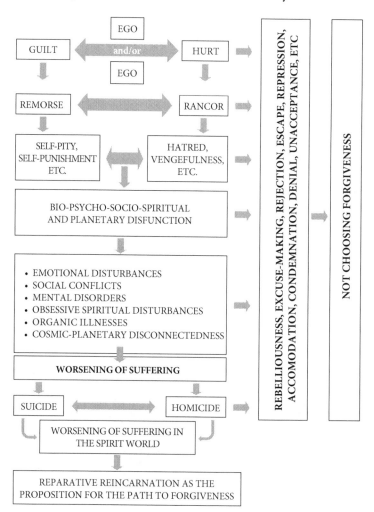

The Dynamics of Guilt – Hurt Dealt with by the SELF

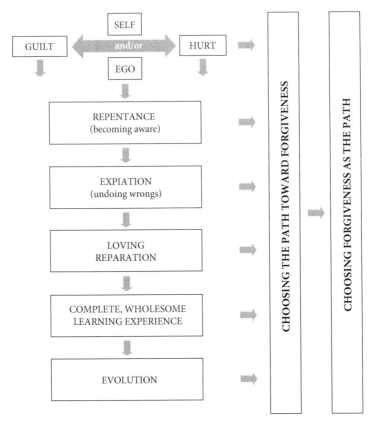

Remarks: SELF = Inner Christ = Inner Buddha = Atma = Transpersonal Self = Higher Self, Divine Self, etc.

CHAPTER 5

LOVE AS THE FOUNDATION OF FORGIVENESS

You have heard that it was said, "You shall love your neighbor and hate your enemy." But I say unto you: Love your enemies...[35]

Love is the basic substance that leads to forgiveness. It is the essence that gives existence and consistency to the materialization of forgiveness. There is a direct correlation: those who love more, forgive more; those who love less, have less capacity to forgive.

For us to understand the dynamics of that love that underpins and paves the road to forgiveness, we must realize that love entails adjectives that characterize its power in various propitiatory nuances of "to give more" in every situation that arises, requiring a greater or lesser amount of giving.

For this to be the case, we should remember the divine conference held by Jesus, which became known as the "Sermon

---

[35] Matthew 5:43-44.

on the Mount." On that occasion, the Divine Galilean proposed the steps necessary for the success of forgiveness and its manifestations in different tones (children): forbearance, tolerance, apology, patience...

The Master intones the beatitudes – whose meaning in Greek is *to progress, to be underway* – in the following order: **Blessed are the poor in spirit, for theirs is the Kingdom of Heaven. Blessed are those who mourn, for they shall be comforted. Blessed are the meek, for they shall inherit the earth. Blessed are they who hunger and thirst for righteousness, for they shall be filled. Blessed are the merciful, for they will receive mercy.**[36]

Hence the platform of love on which to build the monument of forgiveness.

The first premise is humility; the second, tears; the third, meekness; the fourth, justice; and the last, mercy.

The way of forgiveness calls for five loving steps to reach its desideratum*.

* * *

The first step: humility. Humility is fundamental since pride is a huge matrix for non-forgiveness. Pride keeps us from loving because it entangles us in its web, preventing our free mobility and delaying the opening of our heart to life.

Humility restores our connection with the Creator, restoring the flow of love through the Parental Source on which we support ourselves.

Humility enables us to acknowledge who we are – no more, no less: not presuming that we are worth more than we really are, nor deeming ourselves to be useless individuals.

[36] Matthew 5:3-7.

Humility is the opposite of pride, which, due to insecurity, imputes an unreal image of who we are, establishing deformed values, false merit, pseudo-virtues, etc. – in the end, everything that molds false self-esteem. This fragile way of taking our place in the world keeps us far from forgiveness, which demands courage and persistence in order to sort out conflicting content.

Modesty, on the other hand, offers us another way. It keeps us from escaping to the defense mechanism that vain prepotency* proposes.

Humility enables us to establish a more real contact with ourselves. We break away from a distorted self-image, and we connect with our true worth and with authentic goodwill since we realize our sacred origin as children of the Most High.

This perception frees us from the trap of pride, which tries to present us as perfect beings and not beings undergoing continuous improvement; as ready and finished individuals and not as evolving spirits still under construction.

Therefore, this realization gives us energy and courage, determination and perseverance to embrace our failures and, by extension, those on the path with us since we are all students in the school of life, committed to learning from our mistakes and those of others.

Humility snaps the rigidity of pride's coldness, making room in our soul to connect with our emotions.

* * *

The second step: tears.
Ridding ourselves of pride opens the way for the expression of emotion. Pain has a chance to manifest itself

in a healthier way, which leads to healing. When trapped in prepotency, pain becomes silent suffering through an egoic defense that takes refuge behind the armor of non-forgiveness under respectable names: honor, dignity, justice, etc.

No more! Pain can be pain but it does not have to be eternalized as suffering. We no longer need to hide from anyone. We can weep because we have erred, or because we feel aggrieved at heart. We are allowed to grieve without the shame of having been wrong, for we are only learners; and we no longer have to complain repeatedly about having been hurt by someone – that person is also enrolled in the same university of life.

We can weep without crystallization* in pain, and distant from despair.

We can let the tears cleanse our spirit from poisonous guilt, dissolve our resentments and purify our soul of excessive pride...

Upheld in love-humility (easy yoke) and relieved by the exoneration* of accumulated agony (heavy burden), we can keep walking in love in the direction of mercy.

* * *

The third step: meekness.

Meekness is absolutely essential for solidifying the path of forgiveness.

Usually, when we feel hurt, we use anger as the first resource for resolving conflicts. Anger is an almost instinctive aggressive-destructive reaction employed in anticipation of equalizing the injury.

When we proceed in such manner without meekness, we lose any justification we might have had, because, at the least, we are making ourselves like the other person, when we do not go so far as being overly vindictive, going from victim to victimizer, thus reversing the positions in the conflict.

On the other hand, when we are the protagonists of the unfortunate attitude and lack serenity, we run the risk of reacting thoughtlessly against ourselves, increasing our guilt instead of eliminating it. Motivated by remorse, without meekness, we make hasty decisions and say things we soon regret, or we write veritable libels* against ourselves – all because we acted out of anger at ourselves, without the lightness that meekness confers.

When faced with an incident that gives rise to guilt and/or hurt, we must retain our peace-of-mind, especially to prevent an inappropriate impulse; otherwise, we will have regrets and will have to explain ourselves: "I lost my head"; "Before I knew it, the words had already left my mouth"; "I was rash"; "I acted blindly"; "Oh, man! I shouldn't have lashed out"; "By the time I realized what I had done, it was already too late"; "I just couldn't help myself"; "If regret could kill, I'd be dead," etc.

At other times, destructive feelings emerge, saved up from past events that caused rancor and/or remorse, and which are now expressed disproportionately as anger, hatred, revenge... murder; or self-loathing, self-mortification, exposing ourselves to perils aimed at self-destruction... suicide.

In these instances, meekness must manifest as a means of containment (like a mother's arms) so that these negativities do not spread while we work on resolving them.

Meekness does not mean passivity, however.

By itself, it cannot resolve guilt and/or hurt, but it can keep it from getting worse; it does not prevent pain, but it does hinder its fermentation. Lastly, it prevents the entanglement of emotions, which makes the problem worse, and creates an atmosphere and state of tranquility for transformative therapy, thus enabling forgiveness to progress.

* * *

The fourth step: justice.

If someone wrongs us, we feel the need to restore our broken inner harmony as an imperative for consciential justice.

Similarly, our conscience requires us to set matters right when we hurt others.

It is the flow of Cosmic Justice imprinted on our soul, as the Spirits explained in their response to Allan Kardec[37]:

Question: **Where is the law of God written?**

Answer: **In the conscience.**

A thirst and hunger for justice is installed in the soul to drive us to make amends through actual forgiveness for ourselves or for the other person, without inflexibility or lassitude*, without harshness or permissiveness.

* * *

The fifth and final step: mercy.

Mercy is the mother of actual forgiveness.

It is the art of feeling life in the depths of the heart. It means experiencing the sentiment that spills over into our lives. It speaks of a dimension that communicates through that vital center (heart chakra*). It is our sentimental identity, to the point that when we talk about who we are, we hold our hand to our chest in an unconscious gesture of confirmation.

---

[37] The *Spirits' Book*, question no. 621.

Hence, feeling with mercy means enveloping ourselves in compassion: compassion for ourselves, eliminating toxic guilt; compassion for the other person, wiping away hard feelings.

In this instance, the path of forgiveness, mediated by love which serves as the raw material, reaches the culmination of its realization through mercy.

The restorative activities of self-healing begin: self-forgiveness with reparative attitudes toward those who have suffered from our negative, unfortunate action; hetero-forgiveness*, by the completion of the steps on the journey of forgiveness for the person who hurt our soul.

These are actions that restore to us the joy of living; that return us to lost freedom and inner peace; that enable us to assimilate new learning experiences and to proceed to other evolutionary challenges.

* * *

According to all the above, it is clear that the path of forgiveness requires lovingness as the foundation, establishing the five steps referred to as adjectives of love: humility-love, tears-love, meekness-love, justice-love and mercy-love.

There is a deep correlation between Jesus and Kardec, when the latter proposes three movements of the soul to achieve forgiveness. Humility corresponds to repentance; tears, to expiation; and mercy, to reparation. It follows that the dynamics of forgiveness should include these three levels of loving content.

Even though presented in sequence, these steps are not airtight, separate; rather, they must always be combined synchronistically* for forgiveness to be complete.

Thus it may be that even if we humbly accept the difficulty (repentance), we can contain the tears (catharsis*) to avoid the necessary expiation.

Or perhaps after having experienced humility and tears (repentance and expiation, respectively), we may pause at the next step and not let compassion manifest as an expression of mercy, compromising reparation and leaving forgiveness unfinished.

But if we can synergistically articulate the five loving powers of the soul, we will manage to reach the conclusion of forgiveness with its inevitable consequences for growth, lightness, grace, plenitude, peace... Perhaps that is why Jesus ended the beatitudes by stating, **"Rejoice and be glad, for great is your reward in heaven."**[38]

---

[38] Matthew 5:12.

SELF-FORGIVENESS

But Jesus went out to the Mount of Olives. Then, at daybreak {he} went again to the temple. All the people came to him; and after sitting down, he taught them. The scribes and Pharisees brought a woman caught in adultery and made her stand in their midst. They said to him: "Master, this woman was caught in the act of adultery. In the Law, Moses commanded that such {women} be stoned. So what you say?" They said this, testing him, to have a reason to accuse him. But Jesus stooped down and wrote on the ground with his finger. But since they continued to question him, he stood up and replied: "Let him among you who is without sin cast the first stone at her." And he stooped back down and wrote on the ground. Those who had heard began to leave one by one, starting with the eldest. {He} was left alone, and the woman was in the middle. Jesus stood up again and said to her, "Woman, where are they? Has no one condemned you?" She said, "No one, Lord!" Jesus said: "Neither do I condemn you. Go, and sin no more."

The scribes and Pharisees brought a woman caught in adultery and made her stand in their midst. They said to him: "Master, this woman was caught in the act of adultery. In the Law, Moses commanded that such {women} be stoned. So what you say?"

The scene is a dramatic one. The criminal Law of Moses, made more than a thousand years earlier, is harsh, punitive and includes capital punishment – very different from the Law proposed by Jesus, based entirely on education and full of compassion.

While the Mosaic Law, meant to discipline a humanity displaying primitive customs, prescribed stoning the woman, the Great Caregiver proposed eradicating the fault, the wrong, thus mending the woman so that she could shine – the same way as when impurities are polished out of a diamond so that, sparkling, it can be set on a pedestal of beauty.

They said this, testing him, to have a reason to accuse him.

The goal was to entrap him. Acting as judges, they formulated a trap. Whatever His response was, the Galilean would be in conflict.

If He answered in a way that would save the woman from being stoned, He would be in conflict with the Mosaic Law and would be accused with contradicting the greatest of all the Hebrew prophets – Moses.

But if His answer concurred with the great lawgiver – Moses – it would expose the fragile quality of His doctrine, proclaimed as being one of supreme love.

Here the ethics of the incomparable Psychotherapist are being tested; it takes a critical and watchful eye to assess the consistency between what He was saying and the way He was living; it is the verification of His integrity.

But Jesus stooped down and wrote on the ground with His finger.

When someone errs, it is time to be quiet, to keep our thoughts to ourselves. He says nothing. He stoops down, suggesting introspection, self-assessment.

His finger does not point at anyone in accusation. It points to the planet. This leads us to realize that the error belongs to us who live on Mother Earth.

And writing on the ground, He proposes a reflective way. It is the only time we know of that Jesus wrote something.

We can do a free imagination exercise about what He scribbled on the ground. Perhaps a tender invitation written in characters of light for the group that pressed Him, indicating their hatred:

"Meekness! Indulgence! Mercy! Tolerance! Forgiveness!..."

A call to the light comprising us. He stirs up our dormant good side. He awakens our luminous essence.

But since they continued to question him, he stood up and replied: "Let him among you who is without sin cast the first stone at her."

The Greek word for sin is *hamartia:* to miss the mark. The incarnate spirit learns by trial and error. The woman erred in her quest for plenitude, assuming an "un-ecological" approach to her emotional life.

Moreover, Jesus knew that the emotional content of His accusers was filled with guilt, which, in defense, they projected onto the woman, the depository of the pain of each one of them. The persistence of her judges showed how inwardly disturbed they were, because what moves, bothers and hurts us the most often speaks of the pain overflowing from within our soul.

As an expert psychologist, the Rabbi transforms the defendant into a mirror so that each member of the group can see himself reflected in it.

Since He knew about the matrices that drove the group's psychodynamics, he used the Socratic maieutic* on his questioners so that, through consciential self-examination, they could gestate what was troubling them.

Who might be pure enough, thus competent enough, to judge, condemn and execute her?

This proposed a dilemma: throw the stone or reach out to her! Hatred or compassion!

"And he stooped down again and wrote on the ground."
Like a great Group therapist, perhaps He should have written on the ground with His finger:

'What about her co-adulterer?'

If she had been caught in the act, why hadn't they brought the one who had committed adultery with her?

There was an injustice in dealing with the legal part since the disciplinary Mosaic Law prescribed the death penalty for the male adulterer also.[39] Like a fine defense attorney, He exposed a contradiction in that patriarchal society, with its obvious prejudice toward women, and embarrassed the inflexible prosecutors.

What did the man who took part in the illegal act do, such that the woman yielded to infidelity? Did he seduce her, taking advantage of her diseased womanly sensibility? Did he win her over with sophistry*, playing on her insecurity and naïveté? Did he beckon her with deceitful promises?

In short, there was a co-author in the crime; where was he?

'And the husband?'

---

[39] Leviticus 20:10.

Those who care know that no one falls alone. Victory or defeat is always done with complicity.

Where was the spouse?

On that occasion, it was necessary to expand the analysis of the woman's behavior, also including the spouse in the generation of the emotional dissatisfaction that made her vulnerable in maintaining her fidelity.

The Divine Therapist understood that the responsibility should be shared by both spouses and their consciences.

Was she the only one to blame? How many abandonments, rejections and put-downs had she been subjected to while living with her partner? How many times had she been emotionally vulnerable because of his coldness? To how much mental and/ or physical violence had she been submitted?

And lastly, consonant with the husband's conscience, what was his contribution to his wife's infidelity?

By continuing to **write on the ground,** He was inviting the members of the crowd to **stoop** their egos **down,** revealing their weaknesses, their pain; to identify them in order to transmute them.

If during the previous moment He had fostered the emergence of the light within each member of the crowd by speaking to his inner Christ, He was now addressing the negativities, exposing the men's egoic structure.

Thus he was writing generically about the wrongs He was mentally receiving from the psyche of each of them as they surrounded the woman. He did not identify anyone individually, but roused the group to make a self-analysis:

'Slander! Thievery! Lie! Avarice! Greed! Violence! Hatred!...'

And he was picking up on others that were subtler but no less important:

'Resentment! Contempt! Backbiting! Abandonment! Envy! Spite!...'

Those who had heard began to leave one by one, starting with the eldest. {He} was left alone, and the woman was in the middle.

Faced with the woman transformed by Jesus into a mirror, through which they could read what was written on the ground of their souls, the men saw their own unadmitted darkness and began withdrawing – some thoughtfully, others fleeing, but each touched by his inner conscience; the older ones first because they had lived longer and certainly erred more; and then, the rest.

The rebels had come there in a mob, in collusion* but would leave *one by one*, meaning that the group was giving way to an individual, silent movement of introspection, obviously downcast, looking only at themselves...

Only the woman and Jesus remained: symbolically, conflict and solution; weakness and strength; problem and resolution; knot and bow; suffering and love ... guilt and forgiveness!

Figuratively, in the town square of trials, we always face ourselves alone, in an internal dialogue with possibilities for a great encounter: ego and eternal I; human and Spirit; personality and Ethereal Spark, the seal of God.

Jesus stood up again and said to her, "Woman, where are they? Has no one condemned you?"

His focus was the woman, specifically. The others had abandoned the confrontation in order to return to the learning experience of daily life, because they had been fixated on their position as judges and had not come there to be exposed in public. The biggest challenge to courage is to be seen face to face; few are fearless enough to confront themselves, especially in the presence of witnesses.

They had all left, defending themselves egoically. They postponed the encounter proposed by Jesus, concerning their conflicts, their inner complexes, their blind spots*.

They had opted to distance themselves from the Messiah, who would never impose himself on anyone. He respected this and would await their return to the town square of self-encounter.

He dwelled solely on her, who stood before Him.

There was the woman, who could also have taken advantage of the circumstances and left; however, she chose to stay because she knew she was guilty.

No one had condemned her, but she had not exempted herself.

She said: "No one, Lord!"

Jesus had unmasked the "guardians" of morality and had given back to the woman her right to self-encounter. However, if it is true that she had been freed from her external accusers, the same had not happened regarding the inner critic that had immobilized her in the town square of her disarrayed emotions. She was experiencing remorse, of course.

And she lacked the judgment of the One who had stayed behind with her.

Standing before the Master, she was expecting not only condemnation but also execution since He was pure and blameless and had the authority to stone her, according to the Law of Moses.

She stood motionless, expectant, waiting for her egoic guiltiness to be cleansed with the blood resulting from the stones He would cast at her..., or who knows, perhaps a distant possibility: an encounter with His forgiveness, in that she had been able to confront the crowd with the energy of His love.

Jesus said, "Neither do I condemn you. Go, and sin no more."

Hence the supreme Psychotherapist. He does not judge her; He does not condemn her; He does not execute her, faithful to the commandment: *You shall not murder.*[40]

He receives her, highlighting the beauty of His doctrine comprised of understanding and compassion.

He sympathizes with her pain, manifesting forbearance and tolerance.

He goes even further, affirming His lovingness, put in check by the Pharisees and Sadducees, showing mercy through forgiveness.

...Go...

He demonstrates that love loves since it offers new opportunities to start over and stimulates her to move forward, leaving the petrification of remorse in order to try to hit the target by acting differently.

...and sin no more.

As Educator, He offers her the chance to look at the unfortunate incident as a learning experience. The way she had been looking at it had caused suffering.

He supports the woman but does not approve the wrongful behavior that had aroused only pain. He separates the woman from her error.

---

[40] Exodus 20:13.

Nevertheless, He does not reinforce her toxic guilt with criticism and put-downs, which would only increase her consciential pain.

He does not encourage her to remain stuck in remorse; He welcomes her so that she may live and act otherwise, repairing the wrong, the unfortunate act, thereby earning self-forgiveness.

The woman is ecstatic at how He treats her. She knew that, according to the tradition of her people, she would have to face capital punishment; that even if she received clemency, she would be a prisoner of herself both emotionally and morally due to a poisonous sense of guilt, and that she was going to die psychologically.

But He surprises her with an almost impossible possibility.

This time, neither physical nor mental death. She realizes there is a pathway of forgiveness as an alternative offered by the Magnanimous Caregiver; that she would travel that path and take responsibly for repairing the damage caused by her attitude, restoring her right to recover the happiness of living.

And this would only be possible thanks to a new vision – the inner Christ – unveiled by Jesus. From that inner position, it would be feasible to remake the pathway over a certain time and achieve self-forgiveness.

Thus her ego, based on her inner God, would be restructured gradually and progressively, restoring her lost balance.

Jesus becomes the mirror in which the woman sees herself as she never would have been able or dared to see herself. Seeing herself in Him, she feels her inner Christ vibrate at the touch of the external Christ; she sees her own potential for love; she glimpses her divine nature; she recognizes herself as a Flame and, therefore, a child of the Light.

Finally, she sees beyond the human, as a Spirit; she perceives the possibility of transcending her mistake, as an evolving learner; she discovers her potential to overcome her limitations.

* * *

Self-forgiveness[41] entails these steps:

1. Aligning ourselves with the inner Christ.
...you are gods.[42]

This means going beyond the ego to connect with our essential nature.

If we stay only at the level of the personality per se, we will not take the steps to forgive ourselves or others effectively. At best, we will achieve forgiveness *stricto sensu**, that is, limited to the ego.

Depending on the size of the error, the ego does not support or even think about self-forgiveness.

However, becoming immersed in our inner God is not a task to be improvised, or obtained magically through weak, simplistic effort.

It requires systematic, increasingly profound movement, as if climbing a mountain; each and every day, a successive action closer to the summit. The higher we go, the greater the view of the horizon, and the less the importance we give to the tormenting events left down below and behind.

The meaning of the vicissitudes we have experienced on the way up will start changing, and so will the importance we give to the new events we face.

---

[41] *Heaven and Hell*, part I, chap. VII (Kardec, Allan, *Heaven and Hell*, International Spiritist Council, 2006).

[42] John 10:34.

Therefore, the structure of forgiveness will be supported not only on an attitude, when we are faced with a certain negative circumstance, but above all, on a way of living. This is FORGIVENESS, that is, this virtue *latu sensu**, one that goes beyond the ego, including it.

This step, which will be affirmed over an infinite amount of time, must accompany and sustain all the others that follow.

2. Acknowledging our wrong (repentance)
And you will know the truth, and the truth will set you free.[43]

Only sociopaths* do not realize it when they commit a wrong; they are not in touch with reality even when they commit cruel acts. They are psychopaths.*

The liberating path is to admit the truth about our wrong, at least to ourselves.

However, to accept the truth only egoically is to experience self-shame; freezing guilt; fear of the consequences; anger, embarrassment, etc.

The ego will not evolve very much, especially when the pain (remorse) is great, and it will tend to protect itself by using defense mechanisms such as denial (does not acknowledge what it did), displacement (lays its own responsibility on someone else), victimization (acts like an immobilized poor little thing accusing someone else), etc.

On the other hand, the ego can accept its wrongs rigidly, becoming a prisoner of its own guilt, its own jailer.

Whether this or that way, we will stay fixed in the past, consciously or unconsciously rehashing the guilt, experiencing

---

[43] John 8:32.

anxiety about the future, when we expect to reap the bitter fruits of our sowing. Both mechanisms are destructive and thus not healthy.

However, anchored beyond the ego, on our fundamental nature – the Spirit, the ethereal spark[44] – it will be possible to admit the truth of our wrongs (repentance) and despite the pain (expiation), to free ourselves through self-forgiveness.

3. Taking responsibility (expiation)
... to each according to his works.[45]

If we are only driven by ego, we run the risk of becoming immersed in guilt, converting it into remorse, which will crystallize us.

However, if we are in tune with our luminous essence, the possibility arises for us to assume the consequences of our painful acts.

At this stage, the error becomes an expiatory learning opportunity because our remorse has been replaced by repentance, and the error will have had an opportunity to be replaced with reparative action.

Of course, forgiving does not mean ignoring the negative consequences of our acts, which would represent incongruity and inconsistency in light of our past unfortunate behaviors.

Taking responsibility means that we welcome positively the pain that resulted from our wrongful act, and that we change our attitude in order to lucidly and appropriately confront the negative, painful results.

---

[44] *The Spirits' Book*, question no. 88.
[45] Matthew 16:27.

4. Correcting the error (repair)
...let him take up his cross daily and follow me.[46]

At this stage, we are going to rewrite history using new, positive behaviors capable of restoring our self-wounded dignity.

It is a culminating moment because it restores the truth; it is a retraction, a compensatory act; it "cleanses" the dirty deed; it is reparation with regard to ourselves or those whom we have wronged.

This step can be accomplished immediately if the injury was slight, or over the medium or long term if the amount of damage was great, requiring more time to undo the unfortunate results.

This correction of the wrong changes the dark past while creating a hopeful future by a persistent attitude consolidated on the good.

5. Celebrating the victory of self-forgiveness.
Her many sins are forgiven, for she loved much, but he who is forgiven little, loves little.[47]

After having taken the loving pathway that reestablishes inner peace, through actions that repair the damages to others and ourselves, we conclude that forgiveness has transformed vicissitudes into learning, error into experience, negativity into a lesson, pain into a gift, darkness into light – all expressed by a new behavioral ethic.

---

[46] Luke 9:23.
[47] Luke 7:47.

FORGIVING ANOTHER PERSON

And when you stand praying, if you have anything against anyone, forgive them so that your Father, who is in heaven, may forgive you your transgressions.[48]

To forgive another person, it is important to reflect on a few resources that can be used to make the path of forgiveness a bit easier.

These are not steps per se, in that they may be used either sequentially or randomly.

1. Asking oneself: What is the other person's positive intention?

Then Jesus said to him, "Put your sword away, for all who use the sword will die by the sword.[49]

Behind every negative action, there is always a positive intentionality, although it may be hidden to a superficial glance.

---

[48] Mark 11:25.
[49] Matthew 26:52.

It is very difficult for someone who has been injured to accept such a proposition, especially if the injury was a big one.

However, in less serious situations, even breaking the rules and infringing on the rights of someone, the positive intention is sometimes obvious, despite the action being negative, such as when:

– a hungry child steals an apple;

– a woman in a hurry tries to cut in line;

– an annoyed man unloads his aggression by tearing a piece off a decorative plant;

– An elderly man with urge incontinence misses the urinal;

– A late worker who has to punch in "runs over" others who are walking too slowly in front of him;

– A teenager in the elevator carelessly steps on another person's foot;

– A stressed out mother in a small room vents by talking loudly on her cellphone, "wounding" the eardrums of everyone around her.

It is easy to see the positive intention in such incidents, and if we wanted to, we could even forgive the negative attitude of the other because it has to do with less challenging content.

However, there are situations of *magna** complexity, in that deeply philosophical and compassionate understanding is needed to perceive the positive intention behind the negative behavior, especially when it is mean.

The wonderful science of Neuro-Linguistic Programming proposes a way of seeing things that conforms to Spiritist philosophy, when it suggests that we use linguistic keying to scale a mountain of outcomes until we reach a meta-outcome* or meta-intention*; that is, an essential, positive, greater outcome that reveals the philosophical truth that behind every negative action there is a positive intention, even if it is deeply hidden.

We could just try asking about the bad or negative behavior: *what is the good outcome you want with this attitude?* And repeat the same question for the content of each response if it is not yet positive until we reach the positive meta-outcome.

If the situation is simple, as in the aforementioned circumstances, we soon reach the positive meta-intention. Let us look at a couple of examples:

– What good outcome do you want by stealing an apple?

The child will say, "I want to quell my hunger." (This is the positive intention, sought through reprehensible behavior).

Another example:

– What good outcome do you want by pushing the people in front of you?

"I want them to step aside and not get in my way."

– What good outcome do you want from them stepping aside and not getting in your way?

– I need to get to my job on time, so I don't get marked absent." (Hence a better positive intention, although sought using an improper, negative action).

Now let us take a complex, extreme example.

An unemployed man robbed a woman and physically harmed her when she reacted.

– What was the good outcome you wanted by harming her?

"I harmed her because she reacted, but I only wanted to rob her."

– What good outcome did you want from robbing her?

"To get some money."

– What was the good outcome you wanted from getting some money?

"To buy food for my family. (Hence the positive outcome, sought by a succession of criminal acts).

We are not saying what the person did was right, much less agreeing with him, nor are we suggesting that he should not answer for the consequences of his actions, including the repercussions within the ambit of divine and human justice in the civil, criminal sphere, etc.

We are only striving to see and separate, philosophically, the positive intention behind a wrongful behavior, an intention that may be obvious on the surface of a given circumstance; or in another instance, one that may be more or less veiled in the depths of a spirit that has lost itself.

Behind every mistaken, incongruous*, and even perverse attitude, there is a good intention, even though it may be hidden from the perception of protagonists.

That is how we can understand the logic of the psychiatric behavior of a serial killer who murders only women of a certain age group with characteristics similar to each other and to those of his mother, against whom he unconsciously wants revenge for having witnessed, as a child, her killing his father and getting away with it. In the secret corners of his psychopathic attitude, there is a positive intention because he is someone who is trying to end his hatred for his mother and erase the pain of his father's absence, which he has not gotten over since childhood. However, he is mistaken about the outcomes and has made use of the negative behavior of a sociopath.

This way of looking at the matter is an exercise for us and predisposes us to an understanding of others in their inferiority expressed by a range of unfortunate behaviors, such as lies and slander; manipulation and cunning; abuse and invasion; wickedness and cruelty; etc.

Thus we can separate the crime from its perpetrator; the disease from the patient; the error from the person. There is no other ultimate ideal of Justice, Medicine or Education, except to seek, respectively, to stop the crime by rehabilitating the criminal, eliminate the disease by healing the sick person, and correct the error by educating the student.

Within the ambit of forgiveness, we must also distinguish the unfortunate attitude of persons who have hurt us by trying to identify, as far as possible, their deeper purpose, that is, their meta-intention, which is always positive. Thus, even knowing that persons in error will answer for their wrongdoings, we are aware that deep down they are spirits with a divine nature, who have chosen a circuitous route, and have thus acted negatively.

This enables us to be more flexible about the harshness of our judgment, making more room in our heart so that alongside Law there is also Indulgence; alongside Censorship, Forgiveness; alongside Justice, Mercy.

Since the spirit is God's creation, it presents the essence of the same kindness as that of its Progenitor. And even if it is disconnected from its divine nature, it does not lose its intrinsic value; it is like the diamond, which remains a jewel even when buried in the mud.

However rebellious the spirit is in light of the law of progress, sooner or later, in this incarnation or in another, it will return to love, like a sheep returning to the flock from which it has wandered off temporarily.

2. Asking oneself: How have I contributed to the attitude of the other?

Teacher, I have brought my son who has a mute spirit. Whenever it wants to subjugate him, it throws him into convulsions. He foams at the mouth, grinds his teeth and becomes stiff. I asked your disciples to cast it out, but they were not able to.[50]

There is not one single behavior that is not connected systemically with the physical, social and spiritual environment in which it arose.

Every action reflects a choice resulting from interaction with the social environment in which we are immersed. Hence, everything we do is embedded within the sea of influences of those around us.

Thus, when a person wrongs us, we have to take stock not only of those who have contributed to it, but especially of our own contribution.

So, how often do we share the irresponsibility of the other person whom we now feel has hurt us, when we:

– subtly provoked his or her anger;

– provided the fuel for his or her jealousy to explode;

– pushed, with our indifference, a child into the unscrupulous hands of others;

– surpassed, with our aggressiveness, the limit of tolerance of a partner who then retaliated;

– forsook a dear love, thus inclining him or her into another's seductive arms;

– drove the other to rash attitudes because of our psychological pressure;

– contributed, due to our carelessness and negligence, to the ingratitude we now receive from our children.

---

[50] Mark 9:17-18.

And lastly, how many other situations are there, which, though often unconscious but now identified, have made us accomplices in the wrongs that others have committed against us or against our loved ones, not only by the content of our attitudes, but also by our actions?

By the same token, we need to remember the many instances in which our current action, despite being fair and equitable, has not been enough to erase and neutralize the consequences of previous lives, when we made enemies through serious harm, and whose rancor today resounds from our victims' deep unconscious, inducing them to behaviors of disproportionate pay-backs during this lifetime, and only understandable through the law of reincarnation.

3. Putting oneself in the other's shoes
So, whatever you want others to do to you, do so to them, for such is the Law and the Prophets.[51] – Jesus

An attitude of empathy* is an exercise in loving-kindness since selfishness binds us in a position of individualism without making room for other views, especially through the window of our offender. This way of putting ourselves before others results in a narrowing of our vision concerning their behavior, making it harder for us to understand and, therefore, forgive them.

We are more or less limited concerning the truth that we want to appropriate, making us resemble a group of blind individuals who try to describe an elephant by touching just one of its parts: one describes the foot; another, the ear; another, the trunk; another, the mouth, and so on – all with their own truths, their little truths, but none having all of them.

---

[51] Matthew 7:12.

Empathizing with others is not merely a cognitive exercise* entailing cold and calculating intellectuality. It means being able to sense their emotions, emotional motivations, and existential desires. It also means looking through the lens of their education, culture, and history in order to understand their beliefs, thoughts and actions. And lastly, it means appropriating, as far as possible, the filters through which others see, hear, feel and live their lives.

This effort will lead to an increase in our perception, creating a bigger and better environment for commiseration* and Christian compassion, and making the path to forgiveness easier.

4. Asking oneself: And what if I was the one who committed the wrong? Or if I were to commit a similar one?
And do not lead us into temptation, but deliver us from evil.[52] – Jesus.

Have we never committed the same kind of wrong? And even if our conscience is clear, might we not fall to the same point at which the other makes us suffer now? And in other areas, have we never committed wrongs of such severity or even worse? And even if we feel free from guilt and have authority to judge today, who can say that in other incarnations we were as faultless as we are now?

We must exercise other psychological positions in order to open gaps in our hearts shut tight by resentment.

Thus, imagining that we might be the author of that wrongful action and assessing how we would like to be treated, to be seen in a special way, to receive mercy from

---

[52] Matthew 6:13.

the one whom we wronged, and how good we would feel for having been forgiven, would perhaps help us to expand our precarious ability to love, to be more tolerating and more forgiving.

5. Putting oneself in the place of a witness
He said to them, "But who do you say that I am?"[53]
– Jesus

Here is a new challenge in the search for forgiveness – considering a third party besides the other(s) who injured us. This one whom we have chosen is someone who, because of his or her moral authority, is distinguished by his or her superior ability to love.

He or she is a witness, not a judge, lawyer or prosecutor.

This brings up a new perception of reality as a major resource, aiming to enrich our perspective about the incident, and, above all, activate our ability to love in view of the desired forgiveness.

Therefore, it should be someone who "really knows the elephant," at least more than those involved in the problem.

We could choose one or more individuals who meet this objectified standard, someone we know who inspires us to look beyond our limitations.

We could also try to see through the window of a family member who is not complicit in the error, especially the mother or the father of the one who offended us. Such conduct usually leads to a very enriching experience.

After choosing one or more individuals, we must ask ourselves how they would handle our situation and the person

---

[53] Matthew 16:15.

who hurt us. What greater understanding might they bring us? And how might their emotional and moral perception help us? What might their heart lead us to feel beyond resentment?

6. Putting oneself in a place of excellence

I (Saul) said: "Lord what shall I do?" The Lord said to me: "Get up and go into Damascus. There you will be told all the (things) you have been commanded to do."[54]

At this point, we will use a historical personality who embodies a high-order spirit. We are looking for someone who inspires reverence due to his divine attributes.

We will then concern ourselves with reflections, searching for an icon of humanity. For the time being, let us imagine Jesus himself.

If we could hear Him in the folds of our soul, what would He tell us? What might His suggestion be? Seeing through His eyes, what might the quality of our vision be? With what affectivity would He envelop us to help us experience more compassion? Impregnated with His loving energy, how would we perceive the one(s) who hurt us?

This exercise is meant to touch and awaken our deepest essence, which lies buried by rancor and/or remorse.

7. Connecting with one's inner Christ

"You are the salt of the earth. You are the light of the world."[55] – Jesus

---

[54] Acts 22:10.
[55] Matthew 5:13-14.

This is an essential step, which must accompany all the previous ones.

If we remain only at the level of the ego, we will never overcome the offenses committed against us, especially the very serious ones. The ego needs the support and sustentation of a deeper structure and real power – the inner Christ – which has indwelt us since our very coming into existence, when we were created by God.

It is our luminous dimension – the flame[56] – that deifies our existence. When combined with the ego, it structures and strengthens it, giving us enough energy to broach forgiveness in its multiple manifestations, even in situations involving cruelties.

Therefore, it is essential to go beyond social roles, our personality, our biographical history, our reincarnational historiography* in order to access the core of who we are; to make our inner light shine, expanding gradually to promote the evolution that will be affirmed with each incarnation through the expansion of that light, as happens with the potential of the seed that sprouts evolutionarily with every season, en route to its ultimate destination.

Looking solely with the ego is human, limited and fragile. Thus, it manages relative forgiveness at most; the perception of the ego nourished by the god who we are[57] deifies our being, offering strength, lightness, unconditionality, and it promotes complete forgiveness, that is, the FORGIVENESS of God.

Connecting with this original and lasting foundation is a transpersonal search for our trans-humanity through self-knowledge, self-encounter and self-conquest mediated

---

[56] *The Spirits' Book*, response to question no. 88.
[57] John 10:4.

by multiple resources and possibilities, among which are reflection, prayer, the exercising of virtues in general; meditation, cultivation of the good and the beautiful as divine attributes; the experience of charity in its broadest sense, etc.

* * *

Summarizing the resources:

1. Asking oneself: What is the other person's positive intention?

2. Asking oneself: How have I contributed to the attitude of the other?

3. Putting oneself in the other's shoes

4. Asking oneself: And what if I was the one who committed the wrong? And if I were to commit a similar error?

5. Putting oneself in the place of a witness.

6. Putting oneself in a place of excellence.

7. Connecting with one's inner Christ.

CHAPTER 8

FORGIVING THE BODY AND THE BODY AS FORGIVENESS

> And they said: This man (Jesus) said, "I can destroy the Sanctuary of God and rebuild it in three days."[58]

Jesus' statement is excellent, not only for His unusual ability to materialize His own body three days after the crucifixion, but also for His characterization of the body, defining it as no one had ever done with such depth: a *divine temple*.

The body is more than a human work – it is divine; it is more than a house – it is a cathedral.

It starts out with just two cells, in which one (the spermatozoon) is invisible to the naked eye, while the other (the oocyte) looks like the grammatical period at the end of this sentence.

There are approximately 500 million sperm in search of a single egg. The meeting of the sperm with the egg in the

---

[58] Matthew 26:61.

fallopian tube begets the zygote*, which travels to the uterus, where it undergoes cellular multiplication in geometric progression until it composes the embryo and then the fetus (undergoing its onto-phylogenic* evolution), building as many different types of cells as there are tissues to form organs and systems in the constitution of the adult being.

In the adult there are around 100 trillion cells making up the magisterial *divine nave.*

At the foundation of this sublime work of engineering is the constructor spirit and future inhabitant of this sacred space.

Usually, guided by high-ordered "engineers and architects" who help build the work to materialize the body, the spirit abides by a spiritual design that considers necessities and merits, needs and skills, tendencies and purposes, aimed at the best way to make use of the current incarnation.

Like the musical instrument for the musician, the biological body is the raw material for the spirit to carry out its intellectual and moral learning experience in order to attain mastery.

In this building process per se, the spirit selects the available parental genetic material, and using its own spiritual body (the perispirit), in conformity with the laws of heredity, it structures the best (not perfect) body that will serve for its evolution while on earth.

Thus, it is justified in making its selection of a sperm that is not always the healthiest to win the race to the egg in order to generate, for example, XYY syndrome (XYY trisomy*), which entails the victory of a genetically altered carrier sperm over the other, normal sperm. The selection is causal, not accidental.

This also explains the congenital* abnormalities, which are molded on the structuring field of the biological form –

the perispirit – as well as the morbid predispositions that it will imprint on its body, defining the areas that will be most susceptible to future illness.

Consequently, the body, as a copy of the perispirit, reflects the nature of the soul that has reincarnated in it, manifesting, in its form (anatomy) and functioning (physiology), its successes and errors, victories and failures, progress and fixations, virtues and vices, as well as its guilt, hurt and forgiveness; in sum, the entire heritage it has accumulated over many reincarnations.

It was not without reason that Jesus stated categorically: **"And if your eye causes you to err, pluck it out and throw it away. It is better for you to enter life with just one eye than with two and be cast into the Gehenna of fire."**[59]

Thus it is possible to explain how the remorse and resentment that affect the spiritual body are reflected in the biological structure, whether in its anatomy (shape) or in its physiology (function); these abnormalities may appear at conception and throughout all stages of physical life.

Here are a number of infirmities that often, but not always, exemplify such reflections: agenesis* of organs; hormonal disorders affecting growth; congenital alterations affecting a limb; micro and macro cephalism; severe autoimmune diseases; unexpected essential degenerations (without apparent cause) that affect bones, muscles, joints or other tissues, etc.

Such bodily abnormalities are brought over from near or distant incarnations, during which we overstepped all limits of reasonableness with our insane actions, which, thanks to Divine Providence, we gradually redeem, like those

---

59 Matthew 18:9.

who contracted debts in wholesale, but are now paying for them in retail.

* * *

Remorse and rancor promote emotional, social, psychological and spiritual imbalances.

In addition to these imbalances, over time all of our harbored, nourished or accumulated guilt and/or hurt invariably disrupts the biological body as a reflection of the disharmony of the spiritual body (perispirit).

When altered, the spiritual body breaks down the vital body (the etheric double), which disrupts the physical body's functioning and its constituent cellular structure, generating the most varied infirmities, from infectious to immuno-degenerative diseases.

The spirit Andre Luiz describes at length the consequences of guilt resulting in the formation of infirmities[60] (see the end of the chapter "Morbid Predispositions and Microbial Invasion").

The body works like a huge blotter, absorbing the ultimate consequences of unresolved hurt and/or guilt.

Only forgiveness is capable of interrupting the course and direction taken by such destructive contents since they follow the hierarchical sequence: mental body, perispirit, vital body, and physical body.

When the amount of love does not suffice to overcome rancor and resentment, they assume citizenship in individuals and, over time, in this or in another incarnation, they will

---

[60] Luiz, André, *Evolution in Two Worlds*, Part II, chapters 19 and 20, Federação Espírita Brasileira, 2018.

flow into the body as a purifying, painful therapy, instructing the doer of the wrongful behavior that, if forgiveness is not granted, infirmity will replace it.

The bodily vestment is where the resource of the law of nature appears in the last instance, inclining recalcitrant spirits to forgiveness by means of deformities, congenital diseases, hereditary abnormalities, agenesis of major organs, excessive vulnerability to infection, predispositions to serious diseases, significant psychiatric illnesses, etc. In the end, these are the various ways that God's mercy teaches hardened spirits the lessons of self-forgiveness and forgiveness of others.

However, if as rebellious students, we still resist rebelliously by partially or completely avoiding the lesson to be learned, then life will restate such lessons in accordance with our performance and need.

But if we understand the importance of the body as a reflection of ourselves and as a means of forgiveness, we will realize that, due to its foreseen purpose, the limitation and/or the disease is no longer a curse but a blessing.

Also, if we begin to appreciate love as a means to offset their wrongs, reducing or eliminating as far as possible the suffering in general that we are experiencing in this lifetime, we fulfill the New Testament recommendation: **"Above all, however, have intense love for one another, for love covers a multitude of sins."**[61]

The decision made out of love-mercy may interrupt the course of the infirmity, making room, as far as possible, for improvement or bodily healing; or it might paralyze its course, limiting it to being a useful warning, prompting us to be watchful.

---

[61] 1 Peter 4:8.

This is the way a disease's course is reversed, when, upon using the *medicinal substances* of self-forgiveness and/ or hetero-forgiveness, we progress (are blessed) in mercy, promoting health from the inside out, soul to physical body, changing the pattern of our inner energy (fluidic) operation for the better, restoring at a progressive level the harmonious flow of energy to the spirit-body, mental-perispirit-body, vital-physical body communication axis. This also creates a favorable environment for medical and psychotherapeutic interventions, a desirable and necessary synergism* for the complete rebalancing of the being.

At this point, we are invited to see our body-temple as *another* of whom we ought to ask forgiveness for the "ill-treatment" we have imposed on it with toxic rancor and guilt, accepting it as our closest neighbor, thanking and respecting it for the honor of inhabiting it to learn the holy lesson of forgiveness.

Morbid Predispositions and Microbial Invasion

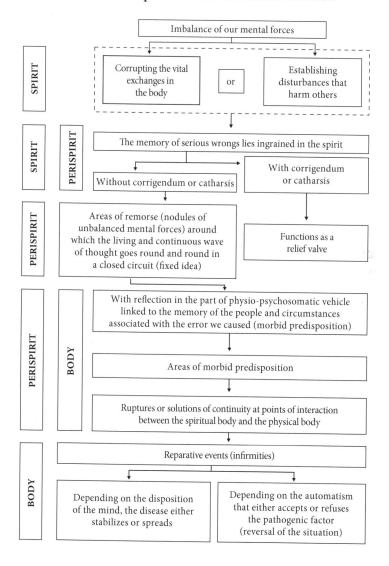

CHAPTER 9

FORGIVENESS OF ONE'S PARENTS

Honor your father and your mother...[62]

You know the commandments: Do not commit adultery; do not murder; do not steal; do not bear false witness; honor your father and your mother.[63] – Jesus.

After self-forgiveness (the fundamental basis for all other types of forgiveness) the greatest challenges to the practice of this virtue generally entail the family, precisely because that is where the most significant people in our relationships are, and, among them, parents are the ones most implicated in this pathway of exercising forgiveness.

This human-spiritual demand has been set forth since Moses received the Ten Commandments. It should be noted that even in a patriarchal society, the commandment

---

[62] Exodus 20:12.
[63] Luke 18:20.

does not say "honor your father" only; or "honor your parents," implying the presence of the mother; on the contrary, it made sure to particularize the parental system specifying "...your father and your mother...", giving importance to both parental figures.

We have an ambivalent relationship with our parents due to our two-fold concept of them: the *profane* and the *sacred*. While we see them as humans – biological – we also see them as sacred – "Gods."

In the human dimension, we bear the umbilicus as a perennial physical memory, pointing to our ancestry; psychologically, along with our surname, we carry the subjective marks of our parents, telling of our history of affective and educational interaction.

In the dimension of the sacred, the meaning conferred on our parents would make them representations of God. And perhaps that is why it is very common to have an idealized image of them, which leads to inevitable problems in the future when we become disappointed at finding out what they are, in reality.

If good parents are rare, imagine how much fantasy there is in the assumption of perfect parents.

We hope for accomplished parents, assuming that they are perfect, but because they cannot live up to such an unattainable description, we are filled with deaf anger, silent resentment, frustration*...

There is a sense of betrayal following this discovery, increasing the relational conflict. Hurt feelings ensue, because we, the children, feel cheated.

However, how can we harbor rancor toward our parents when we have been taught that they are our idols and that we should hold the best sentiments for them? How can we feel resentful toward those who gave us life?

This conflict gives rise to guilt. Guilt at feeling angry toward our parents.

All this takes place especially on the unconscious level.

This is where much of the difficulty between children and parents lies when it comes to forgiveness, for it is here that the matrices (disappointment, followed by hurt, and finally, guilt), upon which other problems throughout life are being founded, in that we do not clean up our history and update the image of our parents.

And if we do not solve these conflicts in time, we almost always unconsciously transfer them in the future to our spouses and then to our children.

Thus, we find:

– wives laying on their husbands the anger they harbor toward their parents, when as daughters they were treated with violence;

– husbands who seem to retaliate against their wives for their parents' indifference at neglecting them in infancy;

– mothers who unconsciously mistreat their children without realizing that it is only the overflowing of pain accumulated from the mortification they suffered in childhood;

– women who seduce and then discard their lovers, without realizing that they are avenging themselves for fathers who betrayed and then left their mothers;

– distrustful men and women who "opt" for celibacy, reissuing the *script* that "marriage doesn't pay," due to what they saw and heard over and over from their parents;

– men who cannot settle into a profession, because they are convinced that they are worthless, following a command from childhood, when they heard their emotionally hurt mother tell their father: "Men are completely worthless";

– fathers and mothers abandoning or overprotecting their children, repeating the pattern with which they were raised by their own parents;

– women and men with low self-esteem due to the guilt they carry because they felt "defective" from being belittled by their parents when they were children.

* * *

We must accept the dual dimension of our parents, articulating it integrally: they are both human (incarnate, evolving spirits) and divine (gods – not Gods – in process of unfolding).

We must deal with the real dimension of our parents, seeing them as evolving spirits, who have brought their experiences over from previous reincarnations: the sum of their achievements and pending issues, virtues and flaws, advances and limitations. They are not gods who have fallen from heaven, nor superheroes manufactured by the media.

Parents and children usually devised a reincarnation plan – not determinism – before birth, designing a project for their bodily experience according to their merits and needs, with the aim of evolving together.

It often entails scheduled reunions for achieving specific goals that are trial-based and sometimes expiatory in nature, considering problems and disagreements from past lives.

It is also true that our parents are not always able to fulfill the outcomes they foresaw before reincarnating, and they often assume detrimental attitudes toward us, their children.

However, the spiritual commandment is categorical: honor father and mother! Whether our parents are the best or the worst; whether or not they have fulfilled their mission well; whether they have loved or abandoned us...

If we cannot love them as we would like, we can at least honor them.

Therefore, we must seek forgiveness, whether for subtle resentment from minor, unconscious negative actions by our parents, or for major hurts arising from being struck by decidedly harmful behaviors.

In either case, on the path of forgiveness, we must ask two fundamental questions:

– What did my parents do to me?

This question should incline us to a better understanding of our existential dynamic, that is, how the areas of our mind, emotion, behavior and spirituality are working.

The answer will give us self-knowledge, enabling us to know the origin and dynamic of our pain in relation to our parental figures, the perception of when and how much they affected us positively and negatively.

That is how we can overcome the tendency to freeze up in dwelling on some of the sectors mentioned.

Gradually, we realize how much we have overreached ourselves in delusional idolatry and the consequent frustrations and disappointments; we can identify the rejections, abandonments and cruelties we suffered in childhood; we can make note of the over-protections, the castrations*, etc.

However, if we get stuck at this stage, we run the risk of fixating in the attitude of victim, a "poor thing," paralyzed in destructive emotions.

Hence we proceed to the second question:

– What do we choose to do about what they did to us?

Here, we make ourselves responsible for our own lives by.

Freeing our parents from blame for our unhappiness and deciding to take a different direction in our existence, having forgiven ourselves for our idealizations* about them, and seeking to forgive them when they failed in their duties as parents.

Reconciling ourselves with our parents before emancipating* ourselves from them so that we will not take our rancor/remorse into other relationships, being freer and more mature for our interpersonal experiences, especially with our future spouses and children.

Praying for them if they have discarnated is another option. Perhaps we can go meet them while we are away from our body during sleep, at a mediumistic meeting, or even reincarnated in the body of a relative.

If they are still in the body, we should make every effort to approach them without violating ourselves, eliminating the walls of defense with which we protected our inner children while we lived with them.

Understanding that forgiveness is not only the cure for the internal wounds we have carried around with us from childhood, but at the same time, the opportunity for treating the pain that our parents have harbored in their souls often ever since they lived with our grandparents.

* * *

A very sick mother in the hospital called for her son and shared a whole string of confidences with him in her death throes.

After she had unloaded, she said to him:

"My son, speak words of love to me that your father never did!"

Very emotional before his dying mother, the son opened his heart, talking about the love she had awakened in his soul and in his brothers'. And while he was speaking, he realized that she had suddenly expired.

Surprised by what his mother had said, and mobilized by her discarnation, he told his brothers what had happened in the hospital.

They all knew about their father's irregular life, but they had never imagined that their mother could have suffered as much as they had inferred during her last confession. She had always spared her children the repeated unhappy attitudes of her husband.

After the funeral, the children, grieving for their loss, combined with indignation at what they had learned, met with the father and patently told him what they thought of him. He had no choice but to leave home immediately.

As the days passed, the children finally realized that they had overreacted toward their father, and had even been cruel. They tried in vain to find him.

The months went by and the son, protagonist of the mother's revelation, felt very guilty, especially because he had been the trigger for the siblings' revolt on that fateful day.

Years later, the children received a phone call from their father in a nearby city. One of the daughters immediately boarded a plane and went to meet him.

The reunion was brief. The father lay dying in a ward for indigents. Soon after she greeted him, and struck by the gloomy scenario, the daughter saw that her father had been waiting for her. He died before she even had time to tell him about his children's repentance.

With this new development, the son's guilt increased because he had not received his father's forgiveness.

Time only made the remorse lacerate his heart even more.

Tired of suffering, he prayed to God repeatedly for an opportunity to rid himself of his remorse.

One day while praying, he felt himself out of his body. He watched as a light-filled woman approached supporting a broken man who walked with his head bent to the ground.

The son was overcome with a feeling of perplexity as he realized that it was his mother, leading his father as if she were a nurse.

His mother said to him:

"My son, neither you nor your father is at peace! You both worship remorse, and it's not doing you any good."

Father and son wept convulsively.

The son proceeded to express his pain to his father and asked his forgiveness for having been overly impulsive and cruel.

The father could only reply with tears, manifesting his suffering for the kind of life he had lived with his wife and children in their home; and also for his shameful flight after having been condemned by his children.

The reconciliation was mutual. There is always time!

Now, the son was looking for a doctor to treat the bodily consequences that his punishment had imputed to him for the amount of time in which he had cultivated the poisonous guilt.

* * *

We make a psychological idealization of what our parents are, which is often far from their existential reality, and over time we have difficulty updating the image we have created of them. It is common for us to crystallize our childish perceptions and to see our parents, for example, as if they were eternally strong, protective and nurturing, even after they have grown old and are no longer strong, but fragile and needy, waiting for their children's attention and care.

Finally, in order to balance the tendency to overstress what our parents did wrong to the detriment of what they did right, it is essential for us to put, on the plate of the scales of our inheritance from them, the positive contents of life with which they saluted us within the constraints that characterized them.

Even when our parents were unsuccessful at fulfilling their duties, it behooves us to look at the upbringing they received from their own parents and promptly realize that they too were victimized.

Thus, from our historical coexistence with them, we will not only pan* for gravel, but also for precious stones.

Therefore, it is essential to enlist positive attitudes, even if they are small and occasional gestures of devotion, affection, tenderness and care; and to realize that even when they errored, there was a positive intention behind it.

And lastly, we should realize that they at least provided us a body for this incarnation. And that fact, by itself, should be reason enough to honor our father and mother by forgiving them.

CHAPTER 10

FORGIVENESS OF CHILDREN

> They brought him little children so that he might touch them, but the disciples rebuked them. But when Jesus saw it, he was indignant and said to them, "Let the little children come unto me and do not forbid them, for theirs is the kingdom of God."[64]

Children are loans from the Creator so that, as co-creators in the position of parents, we may guide them toward the good.

They are spirits at different evolutionary levels, entrusted to us and waiting for the sowing of education by way of love in order to overcome themselves and fulfill the objectives set for them before they reincarnated, and thereby evolve.

Rarely are they souls with great intellectual and moral values already achieved. More often they are spirits of average, if not very limited, evolution, with multiple needs, especially in the affective, ethical and moral sphere.

In certain instances, children reveal physical disabilities at birth or they display emotional disorders or severe psychiatric

---

[64] Mark 10:13-14.

imbalances that usually characterize links of readjustment with their parents, former accomplices of crimes perpetrated in partnership, and now called to the need for forgiveness as a group.

In other instances, challenging behaviors, resulting from the conflicts between the spiritual baggage they have brought with them from the past and the baggage they received from their parents in the present, will only be revealed during adolescence.

And in many circumstances we find spirits that are antipathetic toward their parents, if not their actual enemies, who, from the moment of birth, require the cultivation of a culture of forgiveness to face pending disputes or animosities reminiscent of the near or distant past, and which are made patent in the smallest gestures of family life.

Also common is the reincarnation, as children, of spirits who seriously injured those who are now their parents, awakening in them unmentionable negative feelings, which, only at the cost of much effort can they be mitigated through the daily practice of forgiveness.

How many passionate, emotional triangulations from the past reappear on the stage of relationships between parents and children, demanding, especially from the parents, care in the management of forgiveness for reconciliation, thus avoiding aggravating unresolved hurt and remorse from other incarnations.

Countless other situations lead parents to the path of forgiveness when their children:

– do not return their displays of affection, out of stubborn coldness;

– neglect the educational heritage they have received, acting in head-on collision with the upstanding parental ethical values;

– prove to be ungrateful, relegating their parents to oblivion in the asylum of abandonment;

– profane the family integrity with criminal actions, using the names of their parents;

– usurp and squander the family possessions, without their parents' knowledge;

– fight amongst themselves and with their parents for inheritance reasons;

– etc.

It is also true that there are instances when the parents hold on to resentment because of their own limitations in misinterpreting their children's behavior when they:

– do not live up to the model of children idealized by their parents;

– do not take the professional path that the parents subtly tried to impose on them;

– do not choose to marry the daughter/son-in-law that the parents deem as the ideal;

– reject living in the same house or building as their parents;

– do not educate their own children the way that their parents deem to be the best;

– begin to cultivate different religious beliefs;

– etc.

In any event, with or without reason, it is the parents' responsibility to seek love-forgiveness as a liberating choice in order to fulfill their educational mission on earth, handing their children over to the Heavenly Parent, remembering the attitude of Jesus on the cross in light of the supreme ingratitude of his wards-children, when he said: "Father, forgive them, for they know not what they do."

CHAPTER 11

FORGIVENESS OF A SPOUSE

But as they continued interrogating him (Jesus), he stood up and said to them: Let him, among you, who is without sin cast the first stone at her.[65]

The wife had had intermittent severe migraines since childhood.

Every time she had one, the husband suffered excessively, to the point of being more troubled than his partner, as if he was actually the one with the headache. He would immediately rush out to buy medicine for her at the least threat of running out.

When she would go to the hospital, or whenever she could not sleep at night, he was always at her side, displaying a disproportionate amount of anguish.

Interestingly, the wife would get angry at him at the onset of a migraine, and she would implacably demand his attention and care.

* * *

---

[65] John 8:7.

She finally sought therapeutic help, and she was shocked to discover the cause of her migraines in another life, when she had died from having her head smashed in.

During the treatment, she would see herself after discarnation, hating the man who had caused her that kind of death.

She also discovered that her hard feelings were triggering her migraines.

And that that man was now her husband.

* * *

In view of the problems and conflicts in couples' relationships, developments routinely arise that prove challenging to the stability of the marriage because of the couple's having to deal with emotional injuries, hurt and guilt of varying proportions.

Sometimes such situations are minor and easy to deal with; however, in other circumstances, the amount of pain triggered between the couple is such that it requires a course of excellence on the part of both in order to resolve the issue.

Countless minor episodes, systematically repeated, sometimes crown the years of their interaction, calling for the couple to practice tolerance and mutual patience along the way.

Sometimes, however, there are specific events that represent veritable *tsunamis* that threaten to engulf the partners, drowning them in the murky waters of remorse and resentment, as in cases of severe disrespect, in verbal and/or physical abuse, betrayal, etc. On these occasions, forgiveness is always a need-challenge for both if they aspire to the survival of the marriage and, by extension, the family unit.

Thus, no matter how major or minor the problem, it is essential to evaluate the process of interaction between the one who committed the wrong and one who bore it, aiming to seek appropriate measures for each situation per se, as well as for the relationship as a whole.

Generically speaking, we could see each injury as an offense that has a certain weight (significance) for each member of the couple, and each member usually has different measurements for the same fact.

And didactically speaking, we could catalog these offenses and their penalties, and offer possible solutions.

Following are offenses, with their corresponding penalties (corrections):

1. Minor administrative offense – penalty: a warning.
2. Misdemeanor – penalty: a fine.
3. Serious bodily injury – penalty: imprisonment.
4. Heinous crime – penalty: life imprisonment.

This is not a legal analysis; it is only an analogy meant to lend a better understanding of marital dynamics in overcoming or not overcoming emotional injuries.

The qualification of the offense and the corresponding penalty/correction depend on those involved in the relational trauma, and there may or may not be coincidence in the way both attribute meaning to the same fact.

* * *

It is natural to commit many *minor offenses* in the evolutionary experiences of daily life, and this is easy to understand because one who feels aggrieved also commits offenses with the same frequency. Still-imperfect spirits do very immature things, and words, gestures and inappropriate attitudes become common, requiring the affected partner to exercise his or her ability to grow by means of understanding and indulgence, patience and gentleness, while at the same time issuing a "warning" to the other so that by "paying the penalty" the other can learn and correct him or herself.

A "warning" is a "touch" of love for the other, made using a word, a conversation, an action, an eloquent moment of silence, etc., and it is up to the other to "hear," to receive it in order to reconsider his or her inappropriate behavior and change his or her attitude.

* * *

A *misdemeanor* entails the same dynamic, only it reveals a greater, more intense wrong, demanding a greater deal of effort for the offended partner to accept the other, who must then pay a "fine." This may occur through reparation capable of annulling, within the other, the wrong; thus reconciliation occurs, bringing conjugal maturation.

In this instance, forgiveness takes more time, given that the "fine" will require a lot of dialogue and involve various restorative actions; and finally, it will require a change in attitude until the offended partner feels "indemnified" and the offender's conscience feels at peace.

* * *

When the offense is serious in the relationship, i.e., the equivalent of a *serious bodily injury*, the couple will overcome the conflict only with great mutual effort. These are emotional injuries entailing betrayals, grievous offenses, serious lies, highly disrespectful attitudes, disproportionate neglect, moral and/or physical abuse, etc., which rend the fabric of conjugality with unpredictable consequences due to the profound pain they cause.

Such a time calls for forgiveness as the ultimate manifestation of love. The offended partner is called to hetero-forgiveness, but the offender is also called to self-forgiveness to the extent that he or she seeks to repair the wrong.

Of course, only with both partners' decision to take the path of forgiveness, aided by time, will it be possible to resume the relationship.

There will be a penalty-correction of "imprisonment," featuring a period of time when the couple will invest heavily to restore the mangled sentiment, with the offending partner making a big effort during his or her "imprisonment" to repair his or her conscience, redeeming, with the other partner, the consequences of his or her wrongful act. Meanwhile, it is up to the offended partner to dissolve the hurt in order to open space within that favors a renewed bonding with the same person.

* * *

When the injury is even more serious, featuring a *heinous crime,* separation is inevitable. In this case, the person regards the injury as cruelty, and can no longer find space for trustworthiness and respect, safety and intimacy in order to continue the relationship. The penalty is "life imprisonment," i.e., the death of conjugal love.

But even then – the end of the marriage – forgiveness should never cease being sought as a measure of complete cleansing not only to treat the rancor of the one who was hurt, but also to heal the remorse of the one who was the agent of the cruel pain.

Neglecting forgiveness means creating serious physical illnesses in the future, after the untreated emotions drain into the body.

Without forgiveness there will be roadblocks to new affective interactions, which, even if entered into, the miasma of the wounds still open due to the traumatic separation will continue to be felt.

And, quite often, obsession takes advantage of the resentment and toxic guilt and settles in, immobilizing the individuals who ended the marriage.

* * *

It follows, therefore, that merely choosing to reconcile is not enough. It is necessary to consider three variants involved in the reconciliation process: the size of the offense; the ability of both to forgive; and the time each one will need to walk the path of forgiveness.

Regarding the SIZE OF THE OFFENSE, there may be disagreement as to the classification of the wrongful act: what one partner sees as banal, a "minor offense," the other might see as a "misdemeanor"; what one sees as "heinous," the other might see as a "serious bodily injury," and vice versa. If there is no consensus concerning the significance of the injury, there will also be no agreement about the "penalty to pay," and it will thus require a greater effort to resolve the conflict.

In what concerns the ABILITY TO FORGIVE, there will be differences in the evolutionary level of the spirits involved, reflected in each one's effort to realize a happy or unhappy outcome, depending on their respective higher or lower moral values.

And as for TIME, there will be differences that vary according to the previous two factors. Sometimes reconciliation is immediate, with an apology, because the offense is commonplace; in other instances, reconciliation will require a long time, a long journey toward forgiveness when the offense is serious; and in still other, cruel, instances, there will be no reconciliation, even if forgiveness does materialize with the passing of time; and lastly, unfortunately, there will be situations where there will be no reconciliation or forgiveness in this life at all. The contents of the conflict will carry over to other incarnations as negative karma waiting for dissolution through an increased amount of love.

There will be many circumstances when one will be able to complete the forgiveness (of oneself and/or the other partner), whereas the other will remain mummified in negativity (rancor and/or remorse), preventing the resonance of reconciliation.

* * *

Therefore it is proper to recall the statement of the Spirits inviting us to reflect: "...in short, you shall do for others what you would want your heavenly Father to do for you. Has he not forgiven you often? Does he count the number of times his forgiveness has descended to wipe away your wrongs?"[66]

---

[66] *The Gospel according to Spiritism*, chapter X, no. 14.

CHAPTER 12

FORGIVENESS OF ENEMIES

You have heard that it was said: You shall love your neighbor and hate your enemy. But I say unto you: Love your enemies and pray for those who persecute you, so that you may be the children of your Father who is in heaven, for his sun dawns on the evil and the good, and the rain falls on the just and the unjust. For if you love those who love you, what reward do you have? Do not even the publicans do the same?[67]

The invitation of the high ordered Spirits is clear and indubitable: **Loving one's enemies means to forgive them and to return good for their evil.**[68]

If, by nature, forgiveness constitutes a challenge to human beings on their existential journey, how much more of a challenge is it in relation to an enemy?

---

67   Matthew 5:43-46.
68   *The Spirits' Book,* question 887.

If it is already difficult for us to be lenient with those who wish us well, and to show tolerance to those who love us, then how much more challenging will forgiveness be – as a loving exercise – regarding those who curse, hate and persecute us?

In fact, the difficulty is established because there is a dialectic* correspondence between internal limitations and external demands, i.e., there are intrinsic connections of immaturity and blind spots, which we carry within, with what others present to us, thus giving rise to conflicts in our interpersonal interactions.

Hence we need to reflect on the types of enemies and where they are in order to better frame love in its highest expression: forgiveness.

Whenever we talk about enemies, we instantly think of the people who pose as our adversaries and try to get to us.

However, there are closer enemies that are harder to love and forgive. These are the ones inside us. Those that live within our very being: our imperfections. They hide out and hold us hostage, suppressing our freedom and sabotaging our longing for a happy life.

These are the enemies that violate our integrity, fragmenting us on the inside and imposing emotional conflicts, existential crises, and obsessive disorders, as well as disrupting our social mobility and bequeathing us organic infirmities from the simplest to the most excruciating.

These are the internal "enemies" that connect us with our external enemies and keep us bound to them, preventing our journey of forgiveness. If there is no forgiveness in the "country of our own soul," then expecting us to forgive external enemies is in vain.

It is imperative to love the enemies that indwell us so that we may succeed in realizing our own forgiveness, thus opening enough space in our heart to forgive our external enemies.

* * *

Peter and Judas symbolically represent two possible choices in relation to our pathway of forgiveness.

Judas, dominated by an internal enemy – the thirst for temporal power – sells Jesus to the priests for a few coins after they manipulated his conscience by playing on his psychological fragility.

Then, when he realizes he has been duped by external enemies, he makes the choice to shut himself off from self-charity and sabotages his journey to self-forgiveness. Thus he yields to remorse, opting for punishment in a vain attempt to kill the interior enemy that betrayed him, and, unfortunately, commits suicide.

Peter deals with his inner enemy – his weakness – differently. After betraying Jesus by denying him three times, he comes to his senses and chooses tears as a way to vent his grief. Then he gets up to make a journey of moral realignment, lifting himself up gradually through self-forgiveness, to become one of the greatest disciples of the Gospel.

At the time of his death, the transformation of his weakness into strength had reached such a level that he asked to be crucified upside down, because only Jesus had been worthy of being crucified right side up.

* * *

Jesus scandalized his contemporaries by proclaiming a new and great commandment, until then non-existent in the culture of His time and of His people: love for one's enemies. He dared to declare it two thousand years ago, when today it is still an overly arduous matter to grasp, from domestic relations to international ones.

However, He not only revealed a theory, regarded as a utopian decree, but He also exemplified it in His daily life, demonstrating the feasibility of such a feat.

Because [He] **was the purest being that has ever walked the earth,**[69] He lived at peace with himself, without the presence of internal enemies, and therefore, without the intrapersonal conflicts that characterize us.

Thus He loved those who set themselves up as His external enemies: the Godless priests, the hypocritical Pharisees, the soldier who slapped him, Pilate – dominated by temporal power – and the hateful crowd at the foot of the cross...

He went even further and loved those who had behaved unfaithfully: Peter, in his weakness; Judas, in his delusion; the disciples who slept in the Garden of Olives; the recipients of His goodness, who did not defend Him; and all those who failed to vote in his favor during the infamous referendum that freed Barabbas in detriment of His presence as a pilgrim of peace, condemned to the cross of martyrdom.

He forgave everyone and returned three days after the heinous ingratitude – the crucifixion – to appear to all of them without a hint of complaint or resentful silence; without rancorous blame or a hostile attitude... Just love! Love for His friends and enemies! Let us follow Him!

---

[69] *The Spirits' Book,* comment to question 625.

CHAPTER 13

FORGIVING AND FORGETTING

Jesus said to him, "No one who puts his hand to the plow and looks back is fit for the Kingdom of God.[70]

It is often asked how forgetting works with respect to forgiving.

Forgetting is an occurrence that speaks of corporeal, psychological, and spiritual factors...

Biologically, several factors can cause us to forget: infectious and tumoral, degenerative and metabolic, medicinal and alimentary processes, as well as senile pathologies and physical traumas, etc.

Psychologically, we forget in order to defend ourselves from stormy and traumatic memories; to protect ourselves from emotional threats and aggressions; to face situations involving discomfort and suffering, among others.

Spiritually, due to the influence of the body, we forget when we make the journey of rebirth to undergo a new learning experience; also due to obsessive intrusions...

---

[70] Luke 9:62.

Notwithstanding all the aforementioned instances of forgetting, everything is stored in our spirit by means of the perispirit, as indelible memories that are gradually addressed, dealt with and consciously integrated into our being.

* * *

With regard to forgiveness, forgetting is an event that can be interpreted in several ways.

When the episode is very harmful, we may forget about it since we cannot face it; thus we egoically defend ourselves with temporary amnesia*, repressing the memory so that we are not paralyzed by pain, as happens, for example, in cases involving the rape of an eight-year-old child.

Therefore, in similar events as well as in others of equal complexity, temporarily forgetting is a blessing that individuals choose as the best way to deal with traumas, sparing themselves from taking highly destructive or unbalanced measures such as suicide or homicide, or even avoiding crises that point to mental disorders, etc.

It does not mean, however, that such amnesia is a permanent solution; rather, it is a postponement so that when individuals are more mature, they can find more effective ways of coping with a lingering painful issue.

Thus it is understandable that this sort of conflicting content continues to act unconsciously in people's lives, bringing difficulties and problems until, more matured, they can bring disruptive memories to the surface and treat them.

There are other situations where forgetting stems from the amount of time that has elapsed without our having solved the problem, such that the event has lain dormant over the years. This, however, is not forgiveness, since, if the memory is triggered, we immediately perceive the visible discomfort of the one carrying the bad memory.

We also see reincarnation bringing with it many bad "erased" memories which, due to their unconscious content of rancor and/or remorse, emerge with impressive intensity when triggered by some circumstance.

Lastly, in another interpretation, "forgetting" means using forgiveness to overcome pain reconfigured as resentment and/or guilt. In this situation, the individual does remember the event, but does not suffer any longer and is no longer negatively affected by the memory of it. Upon remembering the painful event, he or she can even smile about it. The pain is over and all that remains is the lesson.

In fact, this is a good indication of how skilled we are at appraising events that had a negative effect on us in the past.

When we recall the event and feel discomfort in the body (unpleasant sensations) and /or emotions (bad feelings), and/or in the mind (altered thoughts), it is a strong indication that the problem has not been adequately resolved. There are signs indicating that the work of forgiveness was either not finished or has not yet been completed.

It is in this sense that the Spirits affirmed forgiveness as forgottenness[71]; that is, "forgetting" means the absence of negative energy (fluid) when we re-encounter (or remember) something or someone: there is neither an unpleasant physical sensation nor emotional dystonia; neither mental destabilization nor low vibratory spiritual attunement. There is only peace in the spirit! ... And consequent serenity in the psyche, balance in the sentiments and harmony in the body.

---

[71] *The Gospel according to Spiritism,* chapter X, no. 15.

CHAPTER 14

BUT WHAT IF I JUST CANNOT FORGIVE?

Then Peter came and said to him, "Lord, how many times will my brother sin against me and I forgive him? Up to seven times? Jesus says to him: I do not tell you up to seven, but up to seventy (times) seven.

Life often entails painful events that go beyond the limits of everyday occurrences.

These dismal circumstances, reported by the media in general, seem to be far removed from our own existential reality, as if they could never reach us, in as much as there is an unconscious rejection due to the amount of suffering they generate regarding both protagonist and victim.

Such nefarious situations arise as challenges to forgiveness, either because the incident is too big for a prompt and immediate solution, or because those who are affected have not yet matured enough in love to handle the injury, which presents itself as hurt and/or guilt.

Thus, as examples, the following catch us off guard:
– the betrayal of a spouse who has always been faithful;
– an abortion, contrary to a family's ethical principles;
– a partner-friend who betrays his company for another, leaving the former in bankruptcy;
– a child's ingratitude, accompanied by physical aggression against the parents;
– an instance of slander that socially stains a whole life of honesty;
– a father who, after humiliating his son, disinherits him;
– the rape of a child;
– a murder;
– a suicide, for which all blame themselves;
– etc.

These and other problematic situations affect us radically, whether we are the victim (mobilizing energies of rancor, hatred, revenge...), or whether we are the tormenter (triggering contents of remorse, self-contempt, self-punishment...).

In either case, it is very difficult to take the pathway of forgiveness.

* * *

If we decide not to forgive, the direction is negative, dark, announcing more, unnecessary suffering.

When we are the target of another person's harmful attitude, there is a tendency toward an impulsive, instinctive reaction in self-defense. This generates a retaliation of equal or worse intensity, in an attempt to "cleanse" one's honor, "save" one's dignity, or "do justice," sometimes culminating in homicide.

When we are the author of the nefarious action, guilt tends to paralyze us, holding us on the merry-go-round of remorse. In our search for "solutions," behaviors manifest that quite often entail escape or self-condemnation, followed by self-punishment configured by increasingly self-destructive attitudes and/or serious infirmities – whether they be physical illnesses or mental disorders – often culminating in attempts at suicide.

In going to such extreme and radically unhappy misbehavior (homicide and suicide), the repercussions may require one or more incarnations until all the devastating consequences are drained and healed.

* * *

But when we choose forgiveness, the course is positive, clarifying, predicting growth and future peace, despite the awareness that we are dealing with an existential *tsunami*.

Of course, after having made this choice, the challenge will be great because it will be extremely hard to forgive the other person or to be forgiven.

Generally speaking, the badly injured person leans toward the immediate impulse of the counterattack. But even by curbing the retaliation, the pain still requires time to dissipate.

Therefore, even if we do choose forgiveness, we cannot usually do so right away, given the intensity of the offense received or committed.

In this instance, at least initially, there is a certain powerlessness to advance down this road. There is a lot of pain for very little love. Progress seems impossible. There is a penchant for abandoning the good fight.

* * *

Spiritism helps us to glimpse how to proceed on this journey. It teaches us the bases for self-confrontation in overcoming our own limits in order to win the victory over ourselves by self-forgiveness or hetero-forgiveness.

HUMILITY is the first step. We must accept the fact that we are unable to forgive (or forgive ourselves) readily. But we must also realize that we have chosen the right direction, rejecting criminalizing ourselves with self-punishment, giving up on nourishing remorse, letting go of revenge and hatred, and abandoning our rancor toward the offender.

* * *

Another attitude is to admit that WE ARE LIGHTS[72] capable of loving just a little more each time, confirming our essential reality as children of God, and consequently that we are gods, as Jesus reaffirmed.[73] And, by extension, admit that we are capable of doing the good that He did and much more.[74]

This certainty about our destiny of deification enables us to advance by accepting our condition as evolving, ever-growing, beings. And even if we are caught up in what troubles us, we can still practice love tirelessly in many other areas of life: toward plants, animals, the planet, and especially other people we do not know.

* * *

Thus, in addition to CHARITY toward our family and friends, we can choose acting as volunteers in the field

---

[72] Matthew 5:14.

[73] John 10:34.

[74] John 14:12.

of social solidarity, selecting among children, young people, adults, the elderly, the sick, etc., a neutral space in which to practice fraternity, thus progressing in our ability to love, like an athlete who trains for hours and hours every day, getting better and better in order to participate in an "Olympic" competition (our greatest problem yet).

Something similar occurs in the art of forgiving the great pains of the soul. By practicing our ability to love, one day we find ourselves capable of greater forgiveness, the kind that overcomes the enormous challenges exemplified above.

Through training ourselves in compassion by means of lesser pardons, in less demanding circumstances, we are qualifying ourselves to perform increasingly audacious deeds of love until we reach the "Olympics" of forgiveness.

This is a true "bodybuilding" of the soul that enables us to use love to cover a multitude of sins[75] we have committed, or of the hurts we have accumulated.

* * *

The use of PRAYER as a means to awaken our inner light will enable us to discover that we are more tolerant and indulgent, especially when we pray for those who have committed serious wrong.

Pray regularly. Neither the shortage of those who refuse to look at suffering – as if it might thus cease to exist – nor neurotic fixation in pain, through continuous, torturous thoughts, must be the pretext for prayer.

Prayer as a means of identifying with God, bathing ourselves in and assimilating His sublimated energies, with

---

[75] 1 Peter 4:8.

which we will gain lightness and peace-giving power in order to continue advancing forward and upward.

* * *

From such PERSEVERING and training ourselves in charity (which is love in expansion) and prayer, we end up by naturally freeing ourselves of the heavy burdens of remorse and/or resentment that initially seemed impossible to remove by a reparative act.

With victory over ourselves comes learning/growth, with which we transform ourselves into different individuals, greater and better than we were before the incident that seemed to be the end of our life, but which, on the contrary, ends up as a motive for another REBIRTH.

* * *

In sum, the six movements didactically interrelated:

1. **Humility:** humbly accepting our limitation in forgiving when faced with the awful pains we have caused ourselves or others.

2. **"You are the light of the world":** realizing that we have the potential of love-forgiveness waiting to unfold.

3. **Charity:** tirelessly practicing compassion in all circumstances of life, and, especially, love-forgiveness in other, less demanding situations.

4. **Prayer:** using prayer regularly, aiming to create an environment that is less hostile or more favorable in order to mitigate negative feelings and bring forth the compassion needed to dilute resentment and/or toxic guilt.

5. Perseverance: realizing that only through continuous efforts in prayer and charity – exercised in less difficult situations – will the conditions for repairing great, unresolved pains be imperceptibly created, thereby forgiving others and/ or ourselves.

6. Rebirth: concluding forgiveness, we assimilate the learning experience provided by the vicissitude – now overcome – and we become better individuals because we are wiser and more loving.

CHAPTER 15

...AND THE WAY OF FORGIVENESS

Therefore, whoever hears these words of mine and practices them will be like the wise man who built his house on the rock.[76]

The Society's [Parisian Society for Spiritist Studies] purpose is to study all the phenomena related to spirit manifestations and their application to the moral, physical, historical and psychological sciences.[77]
Whether concerning historical-moral aspects (laws of love that govern our life history) or physical-psychological angles (laws of love that affect our bodies, emotions, thoughts, etc.), Spiritism has enough power to contribute with other sciences in the treatment of forgiveness.

---

[76] Matthew 7:24.
[77] Kardec, Allan, *The Mediums' Book*, chapter XXX, art. 1 (International Spiritist Council, 2009).

In addition to raising awareness about the excellence of forgiveness as the best choice, the Spiritist Doctrine offers elements for overcoming the difficulties of how to put forgiveness into practice, to concretize it, to make it a behavioral reality.

Being aware of the need to forgive and deciding on pursuing it does not mean we will actually forgive in fact; on the contrary, it is an immense challenge, no matter how enlightened we may be.

Sometimes we have a complete understanding of the dynamics in which we have embroiled ourselves, either through poisonous guilt or through self-grieving hurt. But it is not enough just to be aware of it to eradicate from our heart the shadows* that render us unhappy.

Therefore, in pursuit of this goal we will try to present some resources from the academic sciences, in an interface with Spiritism, in a true alliance of knowledge. In this way we will try to benefit those who strive for forgiveness, but either cannot emerge from the petrification in which they linger, or are stuck on the pathway without completing it.

These are not complex or esoteric* technical recommendations that require, respectively, a helping technician or an initiate. Rather, they are simple and logical suggestions, although effective and capable of being used spontaneously, without requiring the support of experts or gurus.

It is not a question of magical, supposedly miraculous proposals, in the manner of those who rely on superstitions and beliefs. These are propositions that speak of a faith that can "stand face to face with reason,"[78] as taught by Allan Kardec.

---

[78] *The Gospel according to Spiritism*, chapter XVIII, no. 7.

Nor do they represent achievements that require little effort, such as those who aspire to grace without effort. On the contrary, they consist of actions that require a firm and persevering will, for they require repeated, continuous effort.

Moreover, the success of this strategy lies in discipline and persistence devoted to reaching the goal, rather than in giving up after the first apparently unsuccessful attempts, as well as in humility, which will lend its support for facing the pain of pride and selfishness that will soon try to egoically sabotage the victory of the inner Christ manifested through love-forgiveness.

* * *

It is only fair to consider in a schematic way, for didactic purposes, how to deal with conflicting content related to venomous guilt and rancor, as well as with a few therapeutic interventions at every step of the process of healing on the pathway of forgiveness. Such a process will be more time-consuming or less so, depending on each situation-problem confronted, with a view to the preparation, learning, growth and evolution of each learner during his or her spiritual becoming.

Thus we can consider how to handle our negativities (imperfections) and transmute them into positivities (virtues).

The ascensional ladder of forgiveness suggests gradations that speak of the steps that must be climbed toward its fulfillment.

Here are the steps (see at the end of the chapter "The Ladder of Forgiveness"):

a) Desiring, contacting and discovering.

b) Relating to others, knowing and understanding.

c) Becoming aware and accepting.

d) Transforming, maturing and becoming happy.

* * *

A – Desiring to Contact. Contacting to Discover
Question: Could humans always overcome the bad tendencies through their own efforts?
Answer: Yes, and sometimes with very little effort; what they lack is will power. How few of you make such an effort, however![79]

The first movement toward forgiveness is the sincere desire to immerse ourselves in the world of the ego by coping with the problem, using a gradual approach to a courageous contact, without masks, without pretense or excuse, on a journey into the Soul itself, where the true causes of the pain are to be found.

It is very common to completely or partially transfer our suffering – be it guilt/remorse, or hurt/anger – to others, as though unduly "outsourcing" our responsibilities to our parents, children, friends, governments, life, the stars, God...

Thus, discovering these abscesses and our part in generating their true causes represents the indispensable steps to take to deal with our negativities.

The suffering part of our being is like our closest neighbor, waiting within us to be identified, treated and qualified.

Therefore in view of this "neighbor" we must not only identify what is imperfect in it, but we must also believe that this immaturity will give rise to a learning experience (see at the end of the chapter "The Dynamics of Guilt – Hurt Dealt with by the SELF").

---

[79] *The Spirits' Book*, no. 909.

B – Relating to others to Know. Knowing to Understand
Question: What is the most effective means for improving ourselves in this life and for resisting the draw of evil?
Answer: A sage of antiquity has told you: Know thyself.[80]

There is need for modesty and a willingness to take this step, for it requires artistry to live with our psychological shadow and not let ourselves be dominated by it.

The reason is that reconnecting with the same emotions that were buried but not dead evokes powerful content that leans toward domination (self-obsession) due to the intensity of the pain with which such memories are still clothed: either the pain of remorse, which reappears in an attempt to immobilize its victim, or the pain of hatred, which, previously dormant, resurfaces and seeks to dominate those who remember.

Conversely, posture must safeguard the position of those who trigger their memories, ensuring, however, control over their own painful memories. And by ensuring, in this way, balanced access to understanding the causes of their sufferings, as well as to the real motives that interweave remorse and/or rancor, they begin to grasp the psychological dynamics and the way in which these maladies have become structured within the soul itself.

In this way it is possible to deal with the conflict as someone who looks at garbage and sees its potential as fertilizer after proper processing, or as the floriculturist who glimpses the flower that could be born from the muck.

---

[80] Ibid, no. 919.

C – Becoming Aware to Accept
Obedience is the consent of reason; resignation is the consent of the heart.[81]

After understanding the primary causes that structure resentment and/or remorse and their psychodynamics*, at times comprising a veritable subpersonality* – since it can exert its influence and dominion over a person's entire life, characteristic of self-obsession – a new awareness manifests of how to deal with such highly disturbing content, which, if not eradicated, opens the field to spiritual intrusions of a low vibrational level.

This awareness promotes admitting the problem, accepting it fully, if not unconditionally, and enabling the person to take control of the situation.

Accepting does not mean acceding, nor does admitting mean morbid immobility. Rather, it means dynamic control over the unhealthy part of the soul, the part which needs proper treatment.

Usually, it is this shadow (remorse/rancor) that molds the subpersonality, which, if ignored, begins to direct and tyrannize the individual's life by dictating behaviors, emotions, thoughts, etc.

Awareness and acceptance lead to the reversal of this position. By accepting the presence of rancor and/or guilt, the person becomes the sovereign over him or herself, receiving the conflict as a sort of safety container in order to care for and transform it.

---

[81] *The Gospel according to Spiritism*, chapter IX, no. 8.

D – Transforming to Mature. Maturing to become Happy

> (Guilty) are those, who through a transgression, through a wrong impulse of the soul, have distanced themselves from the objective of their creation, which consists in the harmonious cultivation of goodness and beauty as idealized by the human archetype, the God Man, Jesus Christ . – Paul the Apostle.[82]

The next phase is decisive because it is one of change per se. Transformation, maturation and happiness are sequential, inseparable steps.

Transformation implies a movement of the dissolution of negativities, followed by the actions of transmutation, thus establishing positivities, that is, happy learning experiences characterized by lessons in virtue, which are gradually solidified, determining maturity and the resultant happiness.

Therefore, didactically speaking, we would distinguish two synergistically integrated movements: dissolution of remorse and/or rancor, along with positive actions for forgiveness.

D.1. Dissolving remorse and/or rancor

Hence a catharsis of destructive emotions is necessary at the start to rid ourselves of our "heavy burden"; this is the process of venting that will bring a certain level of cleanliness and lightness to the soul.

---

[82] *The Spirits' Book,* response to question 1009.

Let us look at what happens when we eat spoiled foods. The body responds in a wise automatism, using vomit and diarrhea as a means of getting rid of the high load of toxicity brought by the bacteria contained in the deteriorated food.

The same thing happens with the soul as it progresses toward healing. The pains of hatred and remorse are ingested poisons from which we need to free ourselves. Pouring out our heart is a strategy of nature itself, which helps us understand the mechanisms of the physiology of the spirit in the treatment of its problems. Instinctively, therefore, without realizing it, we perform a catharsis of the hurt and guilt by talking about these pains as we breathe (huff) when we are angry at somebody, etc.

Thus, consciously TALKING with someone capable of accepting our suffering without judgment is a good strategy to "vomit up" our pain, purging some of the negativities of the soul.

WRITING, as well as PAINTING and DRAWING, are other ways of releasing our pains, whether dormant or not, which torture us, trapped in corrosive feelings.

BREATHING is another resource for releasing the fluids, the destructive charges that are fixed within the soul, such as remorse, hatred, anger, resentment, etc.

In similar circumstances, WEEPING, as Jesus suggests – blessed are those who weep – and exemplified by Peter after his third denial,[83] can bring us similar benefits, especially if it does not represent a morbid and unproductive fixation on pain.

Sincere PRAYER, made spontaneously from the heart, constitutes a fundamental instrument of relief, for it seeks and finds the maternal lap of God, and receives an immediate,

---

[83] Mark 14:72.

consoling response mediated by good spirits who act by providing a refreshing balm.

WORK, as a useful[84] occupation, is an excellent way to drain off suffocating emotional demands, such as our rage, guilt, hatred, etc., emptying us of the acute or chronic content that might threaten our health.

Lastly, innumerable other activities and resources may be used that facilitate releasing the soul cluttered with "nuclear waste," such as SPORTS, WALKS, PHYSICAL ACTIVITIES in general, ARTISTIC ACTIVITIES, HANDICRAFTS, SELF-HELP AND THERAPEUTIC GROUPS, MEDITATION, ASSISTANCE ACTIVITIES, etc.

Thus, we can use these and other resources consciously, intentionally,[85] to eliminate destructive emotional content, true toxins of the soul, freeing space for revitalizing and reconstructing our physical, social, psychological, mental and spiritual health.

D.2. Positive Actions for Forgiveness

Returning to the comparison with a body affected by food-poisoning, it is fair to consider that, after the relief from diarrhea, vomiting, perspiration, etc., natural abatement is followed due to the loss of fluids and substances necessary for the body to function properly. Consequently, the organism waits for the replacement of water and other vital, nutritious substances, which the individual him or herself, or through external help, provides until the body has completely recovered after a certain period of care.

---

[84] *The Spirits' Book*, response to question 675.
[85] *Genesis*, chapter XIV, no. 20.

So it is with those who have felt relief through pouring out their heart.[86] After this catharsis, it is time for the "hydration and nourishment" of the soul. Alone or with outside help from friends, religious individuals, family, professionals, self-help groups, etc., a loving journey will begin toward the restoration of individuals' equilibrium.

It is not enough to just get rid of negativity; on the journey of forgiveness, it is imperative to build virtues by consolidating the change in the pattern of psychobiological, socio-behavioral, and moral-spiritual functioning.

Positive actions have the power not only to repair correctly, but to promote immunization so that the same slips do not recur.

For all that, it is appropriate to detail a few useful practices for fixing the learning experience in the final development of forgiveness.

All the suggestions that follow are derived from an interiorization[87] that implies self-reflection for self-knowledge, self-discovery for self-encounter, and from self-encounter to self-actualization through the effort of moral transformation.

They are possibilities that adjust synchronously and symphonically on the road to forgiveness.

Some of the resources are the same as those suggested in the venting-of-negativities phase used for building positive content.

* * *

---

[86] *Evolution in Two Worlds,* part II, chapter 19.

[87] *The Spirits' Book,* response to question no. 919a.

DIALOGUE

Dialogue is the instrument for repairing damage and remaking relationships, from the simple apology to the act of reinstating the truth through deep, ongoing conversation. When we use dialogue we are restoring relationships and regaining lost inner peace by repairing pain perpetrated either internally or externally.

* * *

WRITING

Similarly, we can use writing – a telegram, a note, a letter, an e-mail, a will, etc. as the strategy that best suits this or that situation that requires love to advance or complete self-forgiveness and/or hetero-forgiveness.

* * *

PRAYER

Through our thought and will, we possess an inner power of action that extends far beyond the limits of our corporeal sphere. A prayer for others is an act of that will. If it is ardent and sincere, it can call good spirits to the aid of those for whom we pray so that the good spirits may suggest good thoughts to them and give them the needed strength for body and soul. But even then, the prayer from the heart is everything; that from the lips is nothing.[88]

---

[88] *The Spirits' Book,* comment to question no. 662.

Prayer is a most powerful means in the articulation of the forgiveness that generates peace. However, *it is only effective in the case of spirits who repent.*[89]

Prayer is a fertile source of loving fluidic energy, which acts not only on the other(s) who is/are having problems, but also on ourselves. Its action is not just metaphysical or mystical; rather, it implies a conscious, lucid attitude, which also has physical, concrete, tangible consequences, as Spiritism makes so clear.[90]

Whether it is prayer for ourselves, or as intercession for those who have been harmed, prayer is an extraordinarily powerful lever for the objectives of forgiveness when it comes from our inner Christ, and thus sincere, ardent and humble.[91]

On a spiritual level, prayer attracts the assistance of good spirits, and it neutralizes the wickedness of discarnate spirits entangled in the painful process,[92] sensitizing them to the good.

When we pray frequently, the inner hardness of our own heart becomes diluted, as well as the hardness of the other(s) and, over time, it will overcome external resistance to forgiveness.

It was not without reason that Jesus related forgiveness to prayer, when, in the Sermon on the Mount, He points out to us the therapy of prayer, saying: "Father ... forgive us our sins, for we also forgive all who are indebted to us."[93]

---

[89] Ibid, question no. 997.

[90] *The Gospel according to Spiritism*, chapter XXVII, nos. 9-15.

[91] *The Spirits' Book*, response to questions 621 and 658.

[92] *The Spirits' Book*, response to question 660.

[93] Matthew 6:12.

MEDITATION AND VISUALIZATION[94]

> Question – What does worship entail?
> Answer – Worship is the lifting up of the thought toward God. Through worship, the soul draws nearer to its Creator.[95]

Meditation is an extremely timely measure as an act of worship within the format that the Spirits defined to Allan Kardec.

Meditation can be seen as the means by which a person can make prayer a **self-study**, thus avoiding the attitude of those who pray while **closing their eyes to their own faults.**[96]

Consequently, when this resource is used rightly, it can help us discover the blind spots that caused us to fail in our relationship with someone or ourselves. In this way we uncover our shadow part (immaturity), which has contributed to our failure, and we can exit our comfortable victimization or our exaggerated, neurotic self-blame. We assume our active or passive share of responsibility in the conflict that has imprisoned us.

However, meditation along such lines is equally effective in providing us with an immersion in the depths of our being, connecting and causing the light – the *ethereal spark* that comprises us – to emerge, as the guiding Spirits of humanity have affirmed.[97] And in this way, by identifying ourselves with God, we begin to activate the powerful agent

---

[94] See *Life: Challenges and Solutions*, chapter 11, by the Spirit Joanna de Ângelis, psychographed by Divaldo Franco, Leal Publisher, 2014).

[95] *The Spirits' Book*, question no. 649.

[96] Ibid, response to question 660a.

[97] *The Spirits' Book*, response to question no. 88.

of forgiveness through the virtues that emerge from our inner light, facing the shadows (remorse, hurt, enmity, self-punishment, revenge, etc.) to mitigate them in order to attain our inevitable enlightenment.[98]

* * *

REPARATIVE ATTITUDES

Question – Can we redeem our wrongs in the present life?
Answer – Yes, by making reparation for them. (...) Evil can only be atoned for by means of the good, and reparation does not have any merit if it does not strike human beings in their pride or their material interests. (...)[99]

Question – What determines the duration of the sufferings of the guilty?
Answer – (...) the duration and nature of its [a spirit's] sufferings depend on the time it takes to improve itself .... St. Louis.[100]

Restorative attitudes are fundamental, especially when dealing with venomous guilt. When we are taking the above-cited steps in the liberation of negativities, an urgent

---

[98] *A Psicologia Transpessoal [Transpersonal Psychology]*, part II, chap. 14. (Saldanha, Vera. A Psicologia Transpessoal. Ed. Komedi, Campinas, Brazil, 1997).

[99] *The Spirits' Book,* question no. 1000.

[100] Ibid, question no. 1004.

need arises for actions that are the opposite of those that have been harmful.

Actually, it is up to those who have been hurt by the remorse and/or hatred of someone and who identify how negative and disheartening such emotions of the soul are, to repent and realize how they are paralyzed in such sentiments, and thus move forward to forgiveness.

Opening space to establish new, positive, restorative behaviors to the injured conscience is an urgent, irreplaceable need.

Reparative work with respect to those we have hurt, when accessible – or to someone who represents them psycho-spiritually – is an indispensable and inalienable means of pacifying the guilty conscience. Focusing on restorative attitudes that will mitigate our internal debt with which we feel burdened, will, over time, generate an inner indult* characterizing self-forgiveness.

By a similar mechanism, when we put ourselves in the place of someone who has offended us, when we raise the platform of love through compassionate actions toward other difficult people, we increase the inner quota of empathy and tolerance, understanding and indulgence, and we proceed indirectly to forgive those whom we have given the permission to injure us, freeing us from crystallized rancor and hatred.

* * *

SPECIALIZED PROFESSIONAL HELP

Sometimes, help by SPECIALIZED PROFESSIONALS is necessary. Depending on the severity of each person's process, an auxiliary intervention by a professional may be required, whether in the psychological field, through a specialist in the psychotherapeutic area, or whether in the medical sector, with the help of specific remedies and/or therapeutics that are appropriate for each individual.

Likewise, other therapeutic therapies may be useful,[101] under the guidance of ethical and competent professionals, involving breathing, body, music, group dynamics, art, etc.

* * *

SPIRITUAL HELP

Spiritualizing, religious help is a measure that can bring excellent results.

Any religion can be a useful resource if it promotes the moral reform of its adherents.

The **Spiritist Center** offers abundant help by means of the following activities:

– "Spiritual Assistance Meetings," entailing the study of *The Gospel according to Spiritism,* accompanied by fluidic therapy using passes and magnetized water, and fraternal counseling through dialogue;

– "Mediumistic Meetings," mainly those of disobsession, privately attending to disturbing spirit-related interferences;

– "Meetings involving the Study of Spiritism," through regular lectures or systematically in groups;

– Activities involving the "Service of Assistance and Social Promotion";

---

[101] *Tormentos da Obsessão [Torments of Obsession]*, chapter: Terapias enriquecedoras [Enriching Therapies]. (Franco, Divaldo. *Tormentos da Obsessão* – by the spirit Manoel Philomeno de Miranda, 4th edition, Livraria Espírita Alvorada Ed., Salvador, Brazil, 2001).

– Gospel Therapy through meetings of the study and experience of Christian morality, both in the Spiritist Center as well as in the family in the privacy of the home;

– etc.

* * *

CHARITY

> **Question – What is the true meaning of the word charity, as Jesus understood it?**
> **Answer – Benevolence toward everyone, indulgence toward the imperfections of others, and forgiveness for offenses.**

Charity leads us to increase our repertoire of virtues, creating an environment for forgiveness.

Charity is an investment from the general to the particular, from worldwide fraternity toward local fraternity; it is an exercise in affection for our brothers and sisters in general, toward the brother/sister-enemies (internal – something within me; external – someone outside of me).

Whether it is material or moral charity, both synergistically incline us to actualize our evolutionary potential, enabling our spirit to face the most complex and seemingly impossible human issues to be transposed.

Only love in the form of charity can instate humility and enough strength to move mountains of hurt and hatred, misconduct and guilt, opening the way for the reinstallation of happiness by reconnecting us with the Divine.

Thinking about charity, we can paraphrase Allan Kardec, stating that without forgiveness there is no freedom.

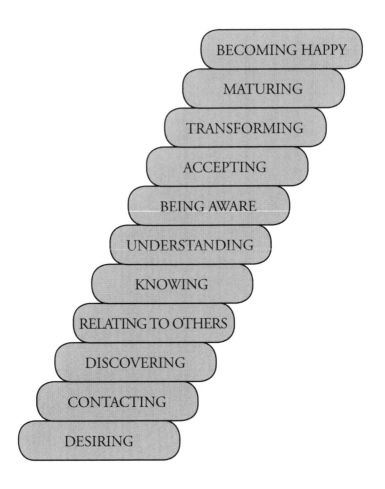

BECOMING HAPPY

MATURING

TRANSFORMING

ACCEPTING

BEING AWARE

UNDERSTANDING

KNOWING

RELATING TO OTHERS

DISCOVERING

CONTACTING

DESIRING

The Dynamics of Guilt – Hurt Dealt with by the SELF

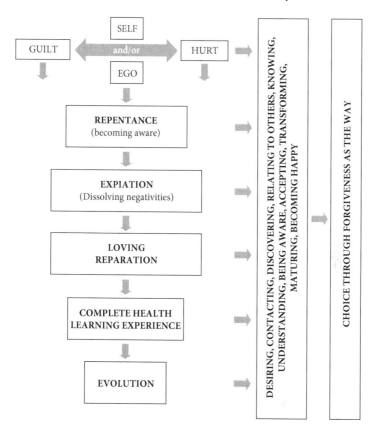

Remarks: SELF = Inner Christ = Inner Buddha = Atma = Transpersonal Self = Higher Self, Divine Self, etc.

GLOSSARY

Agenesis – absence or atrophy of an organ.

Amnesia – total or partial memory loss.

Blind spot or scotoma – in ophthalmology, a spot in the visual field where an image is not formed. By analogy, psychology uses the term to indicate something that someone does not perceive.

Castration – behavior that represses another person's personality.

Catharsis – A feeling of relief from having become aware of repressed sentiments, traumas, etc.

Chakra – In Sanskrit: "wheel," "disk," "center" or "plexus" – each one of the vital centers through which divine energy flows in the different bodies of the human being.

Cesium – Radioactive isotope.

Cognitive – referring to the mental processes involved in perception, representation, thought, associations and memories in problem solving, etc.

Collusion – agreement between persons with the object of injuring or harming someone.

Commiseration – compassion for the misfortunes of others; pity.

Compensation – in psychology, an unconscious defense mechanism, in which the individual compensates for some deficiency through his or her self-image by means of another characteristic, and which he or she then perceives as an asset.

Compunction – a feeling of guilt and regret for having committed a wrong or sin.

Congenital – that which manifests before or at birth; innate.

Connivance – complicity toward the wrongs or errors of someone else.

Crystallization – continuing the same state or situation.

Cupidity – ambition, greed.

Desideratum – a desired thing.

Dialectic – type of logic that interprets processes as an opposition of forces that tend to resolve in a solution (synthesis).

Dystonia – neuro-vegetative dystonia: an alteration in the functioning balance of the sympathetic and para-sympathetic systems.

Ego – the central part of a person's personality.

Egoically – in accordance with the ego.

Egomania – self-worship.

Egotism – habit of speaking or writing excessively about oneself; artificial hypertrophy of the ego.

Emancipate – to set free or make independent.

Empathy – experience in which a person identifies with another, striving to understand what he or she is thinking and feeling what he or she is feeling.

Epicenter – Central point or nucleus of an event.

Exegesis – careful explanation or interpretation of something: a text, a work of art, etc.

Esoteric – regarding a doctrine or system of ideas based on supernatural knowledge or connected to science; occultism.

Exoneration – disengagement, release, disentanglement.

Frustration – disillusionment; disappointment

Hetero-forgiveness – forgiveness of another person.

Historiography – a historian's work of studying and describing history.

Idealization – mental process of worshiping the object of one's desire with exceptional qualities woven by the subject's imagination.

Incongruous – that which demonstrates faulty logic.

Indult – an offering of forgiveness.

Latu sensu – Latin expression for broad meaning.

Lassitude – weariness, fatigue, prostration.

Libel – a written accusation.

Magna – big, important.

Maieutic – name given by Socrates to his dialectic as the art of enabling students to discover the truths already within them, by using a process of multiple questions in order to obtain, by induction of particular and concrete cases, a general concept of the object.

Mask – pretended behavior; false appearance.

Meta-intention – that which is behind or beyond the intention.

Meta-outcome – that which is behind or beyond the outcome.

Miasma – a vapor or foul-smelling emanation emitted by decaying organic matter.

Onto-phylogenic – phylogenic evolution combined with ontogenetic evolution.

Pan – to look for diligently and thoroughly.

Periplus – a long voyage.

Perispirit – the fluidic envelope that unites body and spirit; the spirit's body.

Plutonium – radioactive chemical element.

Prepotency – attitude of feigned superiority; arrogance.

Project – a psychological defense mechanism in which undesirable or unacceptable personal traits are attributed to other persons.

Psychodynamics – area of psychology that addresses the dynamic effects of psychic phenomena, especially those that appear as unconscious reactions to environmental stimuli.

Psychopath – a person with a psychological disorder characterized by a tendency for violent, antisocial behaviors and by the absence of any feeling of guilt for his or her acts; habitually lies and manipulates people. One of the most telling characteristics of such a person is extreme self-centeredness.

Self-esteem – capacity to sense life and be all right with it. Confidence in our way of thinking, facing our problems and feeling we have the right to be happy.

Self-forgiveness – forgiveness of oneself.

Selfishness – tendency to exclusively take one's own interests into account, with no regard for the needs and the good of others.

Sicario – paid assassin.

Sociopath – a person with a personality disorder characterized by impulsive behavior, disregard for social norms, and indifference toward the rights and feelings of others. Has an aversion toward society.

Sophistry – an argument or reasoning that is apparently logical but which is actually false or deceptive.

Shadow – from the psychological perspective – the center of the personal unconscious; the center of the matter that has been repressed in the conscience; tendencies, desires, memories and experiences that are rejected by the individual.

Stricto sensu – Latin expression for narrow meaning.

Subpersonality – according to the Italian psychologist Roberto Assagiogli, subpersonalities are more or less autonomous parts of the total personality, each with its own desires, needs and potentialities. In simpler terms, subpersonalities are the different sides or facets of individuals.

Symbiosis – association of two beings living in mutual benefit.

Synchronistic – relating to facts or circumstances that occur exactly at the same time.

Synergism – cooperative action by concurrent forces, resulting in a greater effect than the sum of the individual effects.

Trans-humanization – "...**man** remaining **man,** but **transcending** himself, by realizing **new possibilities** of and for his **human nature**" (Julian Huxley)

Transmutation – transformation.

Trisomy – abnormal cell condition characterized by the occurrence of an extra chromosome besides the pair of normal homologous chromosomes, causing abnormalities such as Down syndrome.

Uranium – a radioactive metal.

Will – resolution, desire, intention.

Zygote – cell that is formed by the union of the male gamete (spermatozoid) with the female gamete (egg), giving origin to the fetus; egg.

68808811R00090

Made in the USA
Middletown, DE
01 April 2018